ADVANCE PRAISE

"From prison cell to pulpit, Four Time Felon is Rick Scadden's no-holds-barred account of how God rewrote a life the world had written off. Raw, real, and overflowing with hope, it's a powerful reminder that no one is ever too far gone for redemption."
—MATT SHOUP, AUTHOR, SPEAKER, ENTREPRENEUR

"Most of us will never step inside a physical prison, but if we're honest, we all know what it feels like to live behind invisible bars. Fear, regret, shame, financial struggles, broken relationships—these are prisons of the mind, spirit, and circumstances. And too often, they're the very walls we've built ourselves through past mistakes or choices we wish we could undo.

In Four Time Felon, Rick Scadden doesn't shy away from this reality. Instead, he shines a light of hope on even the darkest corners of our stories. He reminds us that no prison is too strong for God's redemption to break through. Page after page, Rick emphasizes that freedom is not only possible, it's promised.

This book is more than words on a page. It's a guide, a testimony, and a lifeline for anyone who feels stuck in a season of defeat. If you've ever felt like your past disqualifies you from God's best, let Rick's wisdom and authenticity show you that redemption is real, and restoration is closer than you think."
—CHAD OWEN, SAFE MONEY EXPERT AND BUSINESS VISIONARY

"Rick's story proves that no one is beyond the reach of God's grace. This book is evidence that God is still in the business of rewriting stories, restoring the broken, and reminding us that our past is a lesson, not a life sentence."

—MATT CRUZ, AUTHOR, EVANGELIST, PASTOR,
HUNGRY GENERATION CHURCH

"I've had the privilege of witnessing firsthand the miraculous transformation of Rick Scadden—a man once defined by his prison record, now powerfully redeemed by the grace of God. Four Time Felon is not just a book; it's a living testimony of hope, restoration, and the relentless love of Jesus. Rick's journey from inmate to pastor is a beacon for anyone who feels trapped by their past. His story is raw, real, and redemptive. I will never forget the day Rick preached a message that led my own son to surrender his life to Jesus. That moment alone speaks volumes about the impact of Rick's obedience and the anointing on his life. I am praying that God uses this book—and Rick's life—to awaken a generation that believes they are beyond redemption. If you think your worst mistake defines you, let this book remind you: God's not done redeeming your story."

—DAVID BROOKS, PASTOR

"Rick Scadden's story is raw, powerful, and dripping with redemption. From the ashes of addiction, prison, and generational brokenness, he reveals the unstoppable hope of Jesus Christ. This book is more than a testimony; it's a lifeline for anyone who has ever felt too far gone. If God can rewrite Rick's story, He can rewrite yours, too."

—AARON LUCAS, PASTOR, CITIPOINTE
CHURCH, NORTHERN COLORADO

"I remember the first time Rick Scadden walked into our church from the halfway house at the jail. From the very beginning, it was clear he was serious about changing his life. And that's exactly what God did. Step by step, I watched Him shape Rick into a leader—a man of conviction, character, and integrity. This book is powerful proof of what only Jesus Christ can do: take a broken childhood, a prison sentence, and a shattered life, and redeem it for His glory. If you've ever doubted that Jesus can transform a life, Rick's story will challenge those doubts head-on. I'm honored to have shared a chapter in Rick's journey—a journey that is still unfolding. This book isn't just worth reading; it's raw, honest, and unfiltered. It pulls no punches and gives you a front-row seat to a life in progress, being daily reshaped by God's grace."

—RICK OLMSTEAD, VINEYARD PASTOR

FOUR TIME FELON

FOUR TIME FELON

FINDING HOPE IN THE ASHES

RICK SCADDEN

COPYRIGHT © 2026 RICK SCADDEN
All rights reserved.

FOUR TIME FELON
Finding Hope in the Ashes

FIRST EDITION

ISBN   978-1-5445-4976-7   *Hardcover*
        978-1-5445-4975-0   *Paperback*
        978-1-5445-4977-4   *Ebook*

To my wife and kids: You are the living proof of grace.

To my readers: Don't wait for your life to fall apart to start walking toward who you're meant to become.

And to Steven: May your name echo not only in memory but in the lives that are touched by the story you helped set in motion.

CONTENTS

	FOREWORD	13
	INTRODUCTION	15
1.	A CHILDHOOD OF CHAOS	17
2.	LEARNING THE WRONG LESSON	31
3.	DANGEROUS FREEDOM	41
4.	THE DOWNWARD SPIRAL	57
5.	THROWING IN THE TOWEL	67
6.	ANGELS AND DEMONS	79
7.	THE BELLY OF THE BEAST	97
8.	STARTING FROM SCRATCH	129
9.	GOD'S CALLING	155
	CONCLUSION	171
	ABOUT THE AUTHOR	175

FOREWORD

—MARK RAMSEY, GLOBAL SENIOR PASTOR, CITIPOINTE CHURCH

OUR PATHS FIRST CROSSED MANY YEARS AGO, WHEN I HAD the privilege of speaking a prophetic word over Rick. I told him I believed God had a great future for him in ministry. At that time, he was filled with passion and potential, and it was clear that God had placed His hand on Rick's life. None of us, however, could have anticipated the painful twists and dark valleys that he would have to walk through before stepping into the fullness of that calling.

Life took a devastating turn for Rick. Mistakes, poor choices, and hardships led him down a road that many never return from. He faced brokenness, shame, and consequences that left him branded as a four-time felon. For many, that would have been the end of the story. But as we know, our God is the God of resurrection power and second chances. He does not define us by our failures but by His redeeming love.

What makes Rick's story so compelling is not just the depth

of the pit he found himself in but the greatness of the God who lifted him out. His journey is living proof that no one is too far gone, no mistake is too great, and no past is beyond the reach of God's grace. Out of the ashes of Rick's darkest moments, God has brought forth a new man—restored, redeemed, and recommissioned for His glory. Today, Rick is a husband, a father, and a pastor, faithfully serving in our church and championing the cause of Christ with passion and conviction. He is living evidence of the truth found in Joel 2:25: "I will restore to you the years that the locust has eaten."

This book, *Four Time Felon: Finding Hope in the Ashes*, is not just Rick's testimony—it's a blueprint for anyone who has ever wondered if God could forgive them, restore them, or use them again. Page after page, you will see how God's grace rewrites stories, how His mercy covers shame, and how His power transforms what the enemy meant for harm into a testimony of victory.

If you are facing impossible odds, battling deep regret, or carrying scars that seem too heavy to bear, this book will breathe hope into your spirit. If you need courage to face your giants, or clarity to find a way forward, Rick's story will give you both. He does not write from theory; he writes from experience—hard-won, grace-filled experience.

I can say with confidence: you are holding more than a book—you are holding a testimony that will inspire faith, spark courage, and remind you that with God nothing is wasted, and no life is beyond redemption.

What a story of grace. What a testimony of hope. And above all, what a Savior who makes all things new.

INTRODUCTION

A DIVINE APPOINTMENT

YOU DIDN'T PICK UP THIS BOOK BY ACCIDENT. I DON'T believe in coincidence, luck, or random chance. I believe you're here by divine appointment—a moment carefully orchestrated to bring you exactly where you need to be, right now, with exactly what you need to hear.

I'm sitting in my office as I write this, looking back on the life I've lived. By all accounts, I shouldn't be here. Statistically speaking, men who grow up like I did—men who experience what I've experienced—end up in one of three places: dead, in prison, or homeless. I was headed down that road, and I had every reason to believe that was going to be my fate.

In fact, I had already been to prison on four felony charges. Society had already labeled me. I was just another lost cause, another statistic. But somehow, by the grace of God, my story didn't end that way.

Today, my life looks completely different. I have a beautiful wife and three amazing kids. I live in a home I used to dream about when I was young, the kind of house I used to work on, hammering nails into walls I never imagined would be my own. I remember thinking, *Man, it'd be nice to live in a house like this someday.* And now, here I am.

These days, I have a job that isn't really a job at all—it's a calling. Every day, I get to preach the Word of God, to help others find the same redemption and transformation that saved my life. I don't wake up dreading work. I wake up grateful, humbled, and on fire to serve.

But things haven't always been this way. I've been at rock bottom. I've felt the weight of chains on my wrists and the cold steel of a prison cell. I've made mistakes that should've cost me my future. I've lived the kind of life that most people don't come back from, but somehow, by the power of grace and the mercy of God, I did.

This book is more than just my story. More importantly, it's proof that redemption is real. That no matter how far you've fallen, no matter what you've done, there is still hope for you. If God could reach down and pull me out of the pit I was in, then He can do the same for you.

So, if you're reading this, I want you to know—you are not here by accident. This is your divine appointment, and if you're willing to turn the page, I'll tell you the whole story.

CHAPTER ONE

A CHILDHOOD OF CHAOS

FOR MOST PEOPLE, EARLY CHILDHOOD MEMORIES ARE filled with laughter, scraped knees, and bedtime stories, but my earliest memory is of an angry man with a shotgun and my mother weeping and pleading with him.

I was four years old when my mother and I were kidnapped at gunpoint by a man I'd never seen before. I don't remember every detail perfectly. Memory is strange like that—some things stay sharp, others fade—but I remember the fear. I remember my mother's arms wrapped tightly around me, her body trembling. I remember her sobs, the way her body shook. And I remember the gun, the way the man holding it shouted, his voice full of rage, full of something I was too young to understand.

I was just four years old. It was 1987. It started at our home, just another ordinary day—though in our house, "ordinary" was a fragile thing, something that could shatter at any moment. My dad had left for work, and it was just me and my mom in the house when the strange man came to the front door. I didn't know him, but he knew my dad, and he had a shotgun.

Apparently, my father owed him money. That's what my

mom told me years later. When I asked her about the incident, she was surprised that I remembered it. She looked at me, startled, as if I had unearthed a ghost.

She filled in the gaps in my memory. The man forced us into his van and took us to his apartment. He kept the shotgun on us for *eight hours*. Eight hours of threats. Eight hours of my mother trying to keep me calm while she was falling apart inside. Eight hours of terror.

At four years old, I couldn't fully grasp what was happening, but I understood enough to be afraid. My fear was for my mother. I watched her cry, saw the desperation in her eyes, and that scared me more than anything.

Eventually, the man's roommate came home. He saw what was happening and, thankfully, called the police. The next thing I remember is my father walking through the door with the cops. The man was arrested, and just like that, the whole horrible ordeal was over.

Except it wasn't. Fear like that doesn't just disappear. It settles into your soul, makes a home in your mind. It follows you. And for me, it became one of the first real lessons I learned about life—that safety is an illusion.

I always knew my childhood was chaotic, but hearing my mother tell this story made me realize just how close I had come to being another tragic statistic. Unfortunately, it wasn't my only brush with horrible things.

My mother also told me about a couple in Denver who used to babysit me and my siblings when I was little. Back then, it felt like we were always being passed around, shuffled from one place to another, handed off to whoever could take us for the day. It wasn't unusual. Stability wasn't something we knew.

One particular couple who watched us, who fed us, who took care of us when my parents weren't around, were actually fugitives. It turns out, the woman had worked as a prison guard, and the man was a convicted felon who had escaped from prison.

Together, they fled, changed their names, moved states, and built a new life.

Somehow, in the insanity of it all, they befriended my father. And then they became our babysitters.

My mother told me she still remembers the exact moment everything unraveled. She and my dad were sitting in the living room, watching TV, when suddenly, the faces of our babysitters flashed across the screen. She turned to my dad, panic in her voice.

"Hey, what's going on here?" she said.

Then the story broke. The police had tracked the couple down. They had figured out where they were hiding, and when they came to make the arrest, the couple didn't go peacefully. A full-scale police standoff erupted, and by the end of it, both of them were shot dead. My babysitters were killed in a hail of gunfire inside the very apartment where they used to watch me, feed me, play with me.

I was stunned when my mother told me this story recently. I tried to wrap my head around it. These people had been trusted to care for me, and they were on the run from the law the entire time. As a child, I had no idea. Maybe it's a blessing that I don't remember. But hearing my mother talk about it now, hearing the emotion in her voice as she recounted the fear she felt when she realized just how close her children had been to danger, was enough to make my stomach turn.

When I look back on my life, it's overwhelming to see the sheer number of times I might have never made it. From the moment I was born, it feels like dark forces have been trying to take me out, yet somehow I'm still here.

A BREAKING POINT

The addiction, violence, and broken love that shaped my childhood started before I was even born. In fact, my parents weren't married when I was born. My mother met my father at a time when she was still quite young, searching for love, for security, for something she thought she found in him. Instead, what she found was a man who pulled her into a world of drugs, alcohol, and reckless living.

Before him, she wasn't wrapped up in that life, but once they were together, the partying became routine, and somewhere in the middle of it, I was born. A few years later, in 1989, they decided to get married. Maybe they thought a marriage license would fix what was already broken. Maybe they believed having a family would force them to grow up, but their relationship wasn't built on anything solid. It was built on addiction and abuse.

I found out later that my father was abusive, both physically and emotionally. That was a hard truth to hear. I never witnessed it firsthand, but when my mother told me, tears in her eyes, I could feel the heaviness of her pain.

"He used to hit me," she said. "He was mean. He was gone all the time, and when he was home, I wished he wasn't."

Dad was in and out of jail constantly. He had multiple arrests for DUI, drug possession, and other charges, and he would disappear for days at a time, spending everything we had on his addictions. Then, when he had nothing left, he would come crawling back home, broke and full of empty promises.

Mom endured it for as long as she could, but there was always going to be a breaking point. That moment happened on Mother's Day. Dad was drunk and being mean, which was nothing new, but this time, something inside her snapped. She jumped on him and knocked him to the ground. After years of being the one who took the beatings, she finally fought back. She was crying, screaming, clawing at him while he lay there stunned. Years of frustration, fear, and rage poured out of her in that moment. And that was it. That was the end.

What followed was divorce papers, court hearings, and custody battles. She thought the truth of his abuse would be enough, that any judge with half a mind would see that my father wasn't fit to raise children, but somehow he won custody. Despite the arrests. Despite the violence. Despite everything, the court decided that we belonged with him. Mom was heartbroken. Losing us devastated her. Maybe she'd waited too long to leave him.

In fact, she'd tried to run before. During one of my father's usual disappearances, she saw an opportunity to get away. She packed up the kids, took whatever she could carry, and left. We went to Pennsylvania. For three months, she tried to start over and build a new life away from him. But he found us.

One day, he showed up again, claiming he had cleaned up, changed, gotten his act together. Maybe she wanted to believe him. Maybe she was just too exhausted to keep fighting. Whatever the reason, we went back with him, and the cycle continued. Except this time, it got worse.

Looking back, I can see how much this affected me. When your earliest memories are filled with fear, abandonment, and chaos, you stop expecting safety. You stop believing in stability, and you start preparing for survival.

BORN INTO A BROKEN CYCLE

Of course, the real origin of my crazy childhood goes back long before I ever took my first breath, long before I was even conceived. The cycle of brokenness was passed down like a curse from one generation to the next.

My mother grew up in a house filled with dysfunction. Her parents—my grandparents—had a marriage that was as fragile as glass, breaking and reforming repeatedly. They got married twice and divorced twice. Their final divorce came when my grandmother flew to Pennsylvania to have an affair, an act that shattered what little was left of their marriage.

It was during this time that my mother, just fourteen years old, had her innocence ripped away from her. She was raped at a party by multiple men, and from that horror, my older sister was conceived. When my mother finally told me this years later, I didn't know what to say. How do you process something like that? How do you respond to the realization that your own sister came into this world through violence?

Mom barely had time to process what had happened to her before life pushed her into something else. At sixteen, she met a man named Randy, and they wound up getting married.

I asked her how she got married so young, and she told me something that stopped me cold. Her parents took her down to the courthouse and signed her over to Randy. At sixteen, she was no longer a daughter. No longer a child. She belonged to Randy. I cannot imagine any parent signing away their child like that.

The marriage didn't last. It gave her my brother, but it also gave her more abuse, more drinking, and more pain. After two years, it ended in a bitter divorce. And not long after, she began dating her ex-husband's brother, the man who became my father.

If alcohol had been her escape before, drugs became her new reality when she got with my dad. He pulled her deeper into addiction, and their relationship was built on partying, reckless decisions, and self-destruction pretty much from day one.

In the middle of all that, she had me. By the time she was nineteen, she had three children from three different men. Three kids, no stability, and no real future.

I asked her once if my dad was present when I was born. She said yes. That surprised me. She explained that for a brief moment in time, he tried to clean up his act and become a decent husband and father. This short-lived effort coincided with my birth, so he was not only there but sober.

Sadly, it didn't last. It never did.

If there was anyone my mother could have turned to, it should have been her own mother, but that was never an option. Her mom had always treated her and her sisters like slaves. There was no love, no warmth, and no sense of belonging.

Mom tried, years later, to reconcile, but it was useless. Her mother never once apologized—not to her, not to any of her three sisters or her brother. So my mom finally gave up, and to this day, they have zero relationship.

For all my father's flaws, for all the damage he caused, there was one thing my mother made sure to tell me. One of his few redeeming qualities is that he took in my older sister and brother as his own. They weren't his kids, but he treated them as if they were. Even now, after everything that's happened, my sister still calls him Dad. So does my brother.

For all the pain, all the destruction, that was the one thing he got right. It wasn't enough to erase the abuse and abandonment, but at least it was something.

MY FIRST TASTE OF DRUGS

By the time I reached second grade, I had already seen more than most kids my age ever would (or should). There was no innocence left in my childhood, just a dangerous amount of freedom and a home that never had clear boundaries.

That was the year I met Richard. We became fast friends, spending the night at each other's houses, running around like normal kids. But in the world we grew up in, normal didn't mean safe. At my house, my dad always had a tray of marijuana stashed under the couch. It wasn't a secret. Everyone in the house knew where it was, including me.

Richard's house was the same. Drugs weren't something hidden away or talked about in hushed tones. They were just part of life.

One evening, during a sleepover at Richard's house, his older brother walked into the room with a joint in his hand.

"Hey," he said, holding it out to us. "Let's smoke this."

So we did.

At just seven years old, I took my first hit. I don't remember getting high. Maybe my little body wasn't even capable of processing it at that age. But something changed inside of me that day. I didn't understand what it was at the time, but looking back, I know it was the moment when drugs became fully normalized for me. That was just the beginning.

The thing about growing up in a house like mine was that there were few rules and no structure. No one was watching closely enough to tell us what we should or shouldn't do. I had too much freedom. It wasn't healthy. I walked to school alone. I went to the movies without an adult. I had no one keeping an eye on what I was doing.

Even though my mother worked hard to keep food on the table and a roof over our heads, she provided very little stability and almost no accountability. And our house turned into a party house every night. People were over constantly—drinking, smoking, getting high, blasting music, and carrying on until all hours. I would lie in bed, staring at the ceiling, listening to the voices and laughter spilling through the walls, knowing that I had to be up for school in a few hours.

Often, I would cry myself to sleep, exhausted but unable to escape the noise and madness around me. Sometimes, I wouldn't fall asleep until one or two in the morning, only to drag myself out of bed hours later to face another school day.

That was my normal.

A GLIMPSE OF PEACE

For all the nights filled with parties, exhaustion, and neglect, there were still glimpses of something normal. They were few and far between, but I held onto them tightly. On the rare mornings when my dad was home—not in jail or at work—we had a Saturday morning ritual. We'd wake up and watch WWF wrestling together, my dad hyping us up like we were part of the action.

He would pretend to be Ralphie the Buffalo, the mascot of his favorite football team, and my siblings and I would jump on his back, riding him like we were in the ring. We wrestled, laughed, and for those moments, he wasn't the man who disappeared for weeks at a time. He wasn't the addict, the convict, or the absent father. He was just Dad.

There were other good times, too—times spent up in the mountains at a cabin owned by my aunt and uncle. We'd escape to Fairplay, Colorado, just west of Tarryall Reservoir, and for a little while, we were just a family. We went fishing, spent time outdoors, and had a taste of what life might have been like if things had been different.

Those moments didn't happen at home. They only happened when we were forced to step away from the world my parents had built and all the drinking, partying, and dysfunction. One of those rare places of peace was at my grandparents' house. My grandmother's name was Edith. She had twelve kids, some from different fathers. The man I called Grandpa wasn't even my dad's real dad. His name was Richard, but we called him "Dick." As you imagine, I thought that was amusing when I was a kid. But when we went out to their home, my life changed. The partying stopped. At least, it slowed down enough that we could pretend for a little while that we were just a normal family.

We'd all pile into the car, drive out to visit, and suddenly, my parents weren't lost in their addictions. They were with us—present, engaged, acting like real parents. We'd go fishing as a family, standing by the lake together, laughing, casting lines, soaking in the quiet that didn't exist at home. And for a moment, I'd let myself believe this was who we were.

But my absolute best memories were the times my dad and I went fishing together, just the two of us. It was our thing. Anytime we were out camping as a family, no matter where we were, we were always the first ones awake. Before the sun had even fully risen, he would shake me awake, whispering, "Come on, let's go." And we'd sneak out together while everyone else was still sleeping.

I lived for those moments. In those early morning hours, outside of his addictions and anger, he was just my dad. Not the drunk. Not the father I had to visit in jail. Just my dad.

We'd sit in silence by the water, casting our lines and watching the ripples spread across the surface. Sometimes, he'd tell me stories about his fishing trips as a kid—the "big one" that got away—and I'd listen, picturing a version of him that existed before the drinking and drugs. We always had a competition to see who would catch the first fish, with a dollar on the line. I always outfished my old man. Now I get to share that same tradition with my son, and wouldn't you know it? He must have the Scadden fishing gene because he now outfishes *his* old man.

In those moments by the water, my dad was the version of him I wished I could have had all the time, and I felt something I didn't recognize at the time. I felt peace. I caught a glimpse of a family that was whole. And every time, as the trip ended and we packed up to go home, I remember thinking, *I wish it was always like this.*

Sadly, as soon as we got back, the world swallowed my parents up again. The drinking resumed. The partying started up. The anger resurfaced. And I went back to lying in bed at night, crying into my pillow, wishing for something different.

Still, those brief moments of peace gave me hope when I was young. They were proof that my father could be someone different, that we could be normal, happy, and whole. However, as I got older, I realized those moments weren't the real version of him. They were just temporary pauses in the storm, and the storm always came back because that was the real him. He *was* the storm.

Looking back, I can see how strong my mom had to be for us in many ways. She was raising three kids as a single parent. Even through all the brokenness, she had a motherly love that I'm still blessed to receive today.

Even now, though, the good memories stick with me. They are some of the few pieces of my childhood that I've passed down to my own kids. I take them to the mountains, to the water, to the kind of places that gave me a brief sense of peace when I was young. But no matter how much I try to hold onto those good times, I can't deny the truth. The bad far outweighed the good.

LOST INNOCENCE

There are moments in life that leave an imprint so deep, they influence the way we see the world before we even know how to process them. Looking back, I realize just how young I was when certain things started happening—far too young to understand, too young to even question it.

The neighbor girl and I were just kids. We played like kids—dolls, house, make-believe—but at some point, our games crossed a line. We didn't understand what we were doing, didn't have the words to describe it, but we knew enough to mimic things we had seen and sensed in the adult world around us.

It blows my mind now how young we were, and how normal it seemed at the time. It wasn't like we had been explicitly taught these things, but we were in an environment where boundaries were blurred and where innocence wasn't something to be protected. We absorbed more than anyone realized, and it didn't stop there.

At babysitters' houses, with other kids, the same types of games would happen. Playing doctor. Playing house. Someone was always the dad. Someone was always the mom. Someone was always examining or being examined.

I look back now and know this wasn't normal. It wasn't how childhood was supposed to be, but in my world then, it was just something that happened. However, something took root inside me during those years. A seed was planted that would grow into a stronghold I wouldn't even recognize until much later in life.

That early exposure to lust, to things I should have never known at that age, followed me. It influenced the way I viewed relationships, the way I processed desire, and the way I understood intimacy. It became a constant battle. Even after I gave my life to Christ, even after I overcame so much of what had chained me down, this was one of the things that never fully left me.

I've been freed, restored, redeemed, but the enemy doesn't let go easily. Temptation still lingers. The past still tries to whisper. And it all started back then, in a childhood that lost its innocence far too soon.

HISTORY REPEATING ITSELF

The cycle of brokenness and lost innocence ran like a thread through my entire family. Generation after generation, the same patterns played out. My older sister was just fifteen years old when she got pregnant. The father of her child was eighteen—legally an adult. Instead of pressing charges, instead of fighting to protect her, my parents did what my mother's parents had done to her.

Just like my mother's parents had signed her over to a man at sixteen years old, my parents stood in a courthouse, put pen to paper, and handed legal control of my fifteen-year-old sister to a grown man.

At six or seven years old, I didn't understand what that meant. I didn't know about age differences or legal boundaries. All I knew was that one day, my sister was there—and then, suddenly, she wasn't.

She married that man and wound up having two kids by him. For a while, it might have seemed like it could work between them, but just like my mother's first marriage, just like my grandparents' marriages, it ended in a bitter divorce. And the same destructive path followed my sister afterward—drugs, alcohol, survival mode.

It was history repeating itself, a loop that no one seemed able to break.

Looking back, I see it for what it was: a *generational curse*. A pattern so deeply ingrained that it felt inevitable, like none of us had a say in how our stories would unfold.

It wouldn't be until years later, through God's grace, redemption, and healing, that I would begin to understand that the cycle could be broken, but only if someone was willing to stand up and fight against it. At the time, though, I was just a kid, watching as my sister disappeared into the same cycle that had swallowed everyone before her.

CHAPTER TWO

LEARNING THE WRONG LESSON

I ONCE ASKED MY MOTHER WHY I WAS ALWAYS BEING passed around from house to house as a child.

"Was it because you guys were partying?" I asked her bluntly.

She didn't hesitate. "Yeah, we were working and partying."

That was my childhood in a nutshell. No stability or consistency, and no real sense of home. I never knew where I'd be sleeping next or who would be responsible for me. Some nights I was at my grandmother's house. Other times, it was a relative's house, a friend's house, or wherever my parents decided to drop me off for a while.

It was a constant shuffle. A life without anchors.

Of all the places I was sent, my grandparents' house in Burlington, Colorado, felt the safest. It was a place of routine, something my life lacked everywhere else. My grandfather was more of a dad at times than my own father ever was. I didn't fully appreciate what I had during those visits. I resented being sent there, away from my mom, away from the chaos I was strangely used to. On top of that, I hated Burlington because it was right on the border of Kansas, a place where tornadoes were common.

I developed a crippling fear of tornadoes during those years. They made me feel completely powerless. I think I subconsciously made a connection: Just like the wind could pick up a house and rip it from its foundation, my life felt like it could be lifted up and dropped into a different place at any given moment.

Not every place I stayed was safe. Some were downright dangerous. I spent a lot of time at the house of a man we called "Uncle David." He wasn't really my uncle, but in my world, blood relations weren't always what made someone family.

Uncle David was one of many adults who took care of me when my parents were out. He also taught me how to shoplift. We would ride the bus through downtown Denver, stopping at Kmart and other department stores. The routine was simple. He would take me downtown to the little strip mall of vendors to shoplift. I would slip things into my pockets when no one was looking: trinkets, snacks, even clothes sometimes. Then the next day, we would go back and return the stolen items in exchange for cash. That was how he made his money.

That was how I learned to steal. At first, I knew it was wrong. I could feel it in my gut. But when we walked away with money in our hands, the guilt started to fade. Uncle David would reward me by taking me to buy something with the stolen cash.

That's how it started. That's how my mind was rewired. Wrong didn't feel so wrong when it came with a reward. I had no idea then that the lessons I was learning in those moments would shape my future in some truly unfortunate ways. Looking back, I can trace a straight line from those early shoplifting trips to the crimes I would commit later in life.

Stealing turned into bigger things. I learned how to rob people, break into places, and get away with things. In fact, one of my four felonies was for second-degree burglary, a charge that carried years of consequences. And it all started back then, in those small moments of moral compromise with a man who wasn't really my uncle.

A CHILDHOOD IN UNSAFE HOUSES

Now, as a father, I see the destructive nature of those formative years. The things I was exposed to as a child became building blocks for the person I would become. That's why I'm so intentional with my own children. They won't grow up in a house filled with partying and drinking. They won't know what it's like to have a father who comes home drunk every night. They won't have to wonder where they'll be sleeping or who will be watching them.

They are safe in their own home. I thank God for that, but I still have fears. Sometimes, they want to have sleepovers at friends' houses, and the moment they ask, I flash back to my childhood. I think about the weed I smoked for the first time at a friend's house. I think about the games we played that stole our innocence. I think about how easy it is to learn the wrong lessons from the wrong people. And I struggle because I know what happened to me. I don't ever want it to happen to them.

The parties never stopped. Every single night, our house was filled with noise, chaos, and people who didn't care that kids were trying to sleep in the next room. Some nights it was all laughter, cheers, and music blasting, but other nights—the bad nights—there was screaming, yelling, and fights that felt like they'd never end.

As a kid, all I could do was lie in bed and cry, frustrated and completely exhausted, but I was the youngest in a family of five—I didn't have a voice. I couldn't go out there and tell the adults to shut up and go home. I tried, sometimes. I remember screaming, "Be quiet!" but no one ever listened. I was just a kid, and they were drunk, high, and lost in their own world.

The parties bled into the mornings, especially on weekends. Some nights they drank until the sun came up, and I would get up for school or wake up on a Saturday morning to find the house still full of people, passed out in corners, sprawled on couches, cigarette butts and beer bottles littering the floor.

To this day, I'm a light sleeper because of it. Every noise in the night startles me awake, heart pounding, mind racing. When I get woken up suddenly, I feel anger flare inside me before I even know why. It's all those years of being forced to listen to chaos when all I wanted was peace.

One year, the partying didn't just steal my sleep. It stole Christmas.

I woke up early, excited like every kid should be on Christmas morning, but when I ran into the living room, I saw something was wrong. The stockings were empty, and the presents were nowhere to be found.

I ran to my dad's room and shook him awake. "Dad, you forgot to put out the presents! You forgot the stockings!"

He groggily got up, still hungover, fumbling to fix it. Watching him try to pull Christmas together last-minute was worse than if there had been no presents at all. I felt bad for him. Even as a kid, I knew he was drowning in his own addictions.

I shouldn't have had to wake him up that morning. I shouldn't have had to feel sorry for my father. I shouldn't have had to raise myself while he drowned. But that's what growing up in that house was like.

Even Christmas wasn't safe from the addiction and partying, and the neglect that came with it.

VISITING DAD IN JAIL

My father was in and out of jail a lot when I was a child. I have vivid memories of visiting him behind bars, and every time it felt like a rerun of the same sad story. I remember standing in the cold for hours, waiting outside for the jail doors to open. Sometimes, my hands would be so frozen that I'd ball them into fists in my coat pockets, trying to keep warm.

When we finally got inside and saw him, there was always this strange contrast between my father and his environment.

He always looked healthy. That was the thing about seeing him in jail. He was sober, his eyes were clearer, his face wasn't sunken in, and he wasn't skinny from going days without eating, drinking, or taking care of himself. He looked stronger, more like a real dad.

It's messed up to admit, but sometimes I felt relief knowing he was there. At least in jail, he wasn't drinking himself to death. At least in jail, he wasn't high.

But for my mom, there was no silver lining. The burden of it all fell on her. "Here we are again," she would mutter under her breath, eyes red from crying, voice tight with exhaustion.

While my dad sat in a cell, serving time for whatever he had done this time, she had to pay the rent, put food on the table, and take care of us alone. When she couldn't do it alone, my grandma stepped in. Sometimes Grandma stayed with us for weeks, even months, to help keep things together.

I remember standing in line with my mom at the Social Security office, the welfare office, waiting for food stamps. This was back when they gave you a book of paper stamps, before everything switched to cards. We would stand in line for government food boxes, picking up whatever supplies they handed out: blocks of cheese, powdered milk, cans of mystery meat.

And when my dad finally got out, nothing changed. We were still poor, still living on food stamps, and still struggling. Still waiting for the next time we'd be back in that line, waiting outside those jail doors again.

CINNAMON ROLLS IN GRANDMA'S KITCHEN

Like I said, my grandma's house in Burlington was the only place where I felt safe enough to relax. Unfortunately, I also had enough space and freedom to get into trouble.

One time, I got caught shoplifting at a small store downtown. It wasn't my first time at that particular location. I had been stealing from the local drugstore for a while, pulling the same scam my uncle taught me back in Denver. I would take something off the shelf, walk up to the counter, pretend I had bought it earlier, and return it for cash.

It was easy money, until I got caught.

I don't even remember the punishment. I just remember the shame, a feeling of knowing I had done wrong but not really knowing how to stop. Since stealing had been introduced to me so early, it didn't feel like crime. It felt like a strange survival tactic.

Still, for all the trouble I got into out there, some of my best memories were in my grandma's kitchen. She made the best cinnamon rolls. I would stand next to her, watching as she rolled out the dough, sprinkled the cinnamon and sugar, and carefully twisted each roll into shape. The smell of butter and brown sugar would fill the whole house as they baked, and when they came out of the oven, she'd drizzle the icing while they were still warm.

Life in my grandmother's house was so different from my everyday life. There was no yelling, no fighting, no drunken chaos—just warmth, the smell of cinnamon, and the feeling of being wanted. For a kid growing up in constant instability, those moments felt magical.

The thing is, I didn't know my "normal" life was so abnormal. My parents partied, drank, and did drugs, but so did my friends' parents. My best friend Richard's house was just like mine. There was noise, chaos, and people coming and going at all hours.

It wasn't until I got older that I started to question it. I started to see other families who didn't live like we did, who didn't have to visit their dads in jail, who didn't have to sleep through all-night parties or wake up to empty refrigerators. I started to see that what I thought was normal wasn't.

To be fair, my father didn't have a father of his own. He learned how to be a man by watching his older brothers and seeing how men treated his mom, and that's what he passed down to us. My parents were so young. I don't blame them for what they didn't know. They were trying to raise us with the only tools they had been given, and those tools were broken.

They had nothing to draw from, no blueprint for how to raise a family the right way. And yet, in the middle of all the madness, I still had cinnamon rolls in Grandma's kitchen. Those little moments of stability, of what could have been, are what I now fight to give my own kids.

THE WEIGHT OF GROWING UP TOO SOON

I remember walking alone to school every morning. My mother insists that my older brother walked with me, but I don't have a single memory of him by my side. What's burned in my mind is walking alone, navigating the cracked sidewalks and quiet, sometimes menacing streets.

The path was simple—down the street, take a right, and I'd reach the school—but simple doesn't mean safe. Even if my brother had walked with me, what did that really change? He was only nine, and I was seven. We were two kids who should've had someone looking out for us, but we didn't.

I also remember walking to the movies by myself. In fact, I often wandered the neighborhood alone. At the time, it didn't strike me as odd. It was just life. But now, when I look back at that neighborhood, at those streets, I wonder how I made it out. The place wasn't safe then, and it's worse now. I could've been taken, hurt, or lost in a system that swallowed up kids like me, but somehow, I survived.

My mom did her best; I believe that now. There was always food on the table and a roof over our heads, even in the midst of chaos and instability. But I also learned early what *not* to do. I learned that men weren't supposed to hit women—a lesson my mother learned the hard way. She taught me that no matter what, abuse was wrong, but by the time I understood that, I had already seen too much of it.

I also learned what a strong work ethic looks like. My dad, for all his failings, had an almost inhuman ability to party all night, drink until he was barely standing, and still get up and go to work the next morning. I don't know how he did it. Maybe he was still drunk when he clocked in, but he worked. That stayed with me. No matter how broken your life is, you get up and do what you have to do. That was one of the few things I ever took from my father.

Still, by second grade, I was already angry and acting out. I threw rocks at kids during recess. One of them hit a boy in the head and split it open. I lied and said I thought it was just a piece of dirt, but they saw through it. At just seven years old, I got suspended from school.

I also had a girlfriend. We even kissed. That might seem innocent, but it was just another sign of how early I was exposed to things I shouldn't have known about yet.

I was doing stupid things all the time, but I wasn't trying to be bad. I was acting out because I didn't know what to do with everything I was feeling. I was angry, lost, and hurt, and no one noticed. No one pulled me aside and asked, "What's wrong?" No one wondered why a kid who should have been worried about cartoons and recess was instead fighting, lying, and getting suspended.

I established a pattern of lashing out instead of expressing my emotions. I was already on a path that, if something didn't change, would lead me exactly where I ended up—a convict, a felon, locked away like so many others who never got the chance to break the cycle.

People like to say, "The past is the past." They think that what happens in childhood stays there, buried under time, but that's not true. Trauma doesn't disappear. It doesn't vanish just because you grow up. It follows you. It seeps into your habits, your choices, your relationships. It twists the way you see the world.

Healing doesn't mean forgetting. Healing means *unpeeling*. The more layers you pull back, the more you realize how deeply embedded the pain is. You deal with one thing only to uncover another wound beneath it. And another. And another.

I'm still peeling back layers. Still facing the deep hurt of a childhood where I learned the wrong things too early and the right things too late. Maybe that's why I'm writing this book now, because if someone had recognized the anger in a seven-year-old boy, if someone had seen the pain in the way I acted out, maybe things could have been different. Maybe. But I can't change what was. I can only keep peeling back the layers and choosing a different path now.

CHAPTER THREE

DANGEROUS FREEDOM

BY THIRD GRADE, I FOUND MYSELF IN A WORLD THAT didn't make sense anymore. My parents divorced, and everything familiar unraveled all at once. We moved into a house my dad was renting, but it didn't feel like a home. It was more like a shelter where the echoes of our old life faded behind new walls.

Life without my parents together felt foreign, like walking around in shoes that didn't fit. My dad was trying, I could tell. He worked hard to provide for us, pulling together the broken pieces in his own way, and on weekends he'd make attempts at normalcy. Sometimes he'd take us up to the mountains, renting a cheap hotel near Estes Park so we could go fishing or skip stones across the lake like nothing had changed.

Those brief trips felt sacred, moments when we escaped just enough to remember what family felt like. Sitting in a canoe or feeling the tug of a trout on the line, I saw my dad trying to reclaim fatherhood, maybe even himself. I still hold onto those moments. Fleeting as they were, they were lovely.

But everything had changed. There was no denying it.

Around this time, Paula came into our lives. Dad met her

during a stint in jail, and when she got out, she moved in with us, bringing her daughter, Marissa, along. That's when the experiment of a blended family began.

It didn't go well. Paula wasn't a healthy influence. She drank and used as much as my dad did, maybe more. She constantly tore him down, and he let her do it. They fed off each other's brokenness. Our home was filled with more tension than peace. They fought a lot, but in their own broken way, they clearly loved each other. It was an atmosphere of addiction and unspoken pain. As a kid, I didn't fully understand the dynamics, but I felt them in my bones.

Dad wanted to start over, I think. He wanted to rebuild his life after the divorce, but alcohol, drugs, and disappointment were bears on his back. They took his money, his time, and slowly, they took all of him.

As for me, the divorce hit deeper than I understood at the time. It created this illusion of freedom that turned out to be dangerous. I learned how to manipulate the space between two households. I would exploit the bitterness between my parents by telling one what the other allowed, bending rules, and becoming someone different depending on where I was. It gave me a false sense of control in a world that felt out of control.

Eventually, my dad had two more daughters with Paula: Rochelle and Kathryn. They were half sisters by blood, but full sisters in every way that matters. I'm still close with all three girls, including Marissa, but even those relationships carry scars. What those girls had to go through was heartbreaking, and it shaped all of us in ways we're still untangling.

Looking back at my dad, I see a man who wanted to be a father and a family man, who tried to reach for the good but couldn't shake what was gripping him. And I see a boy—me—trying to find peace between two worlds and learning to survive in the in-between.

EVERYTHING UNRAVELS

A new house in a new neighborhood was a fresh start on paper, but it wasn't long before I realized we hadn't left the chaos behind. If anything, we had just stepped into a different kind of storm.

There was a family across the street that looked a lot like ours: three kids, a dad, a home full of noise. But behind closed doors, it was utter mayhem. There was drugs, alcohol, and rampant abuse. Their father was growing marijuana right there in the house, and his anger ran deeper than the roots of the weed in his basement. He hit his kids all the time. I know because I heard screaming.

Somehow, despite all of this, our families became friends.

It didn't take long before their dysfunction started to bleed into our own. That's where I took my first sip of alcohol—boxed wine, stolen from our basement. I had my first cigarette. My second hit of weed (but the first time I actually got high). At eight years old, I was sitting on a torn-up couch in a dark basement, inhaling the smoke from a stash we'd taken from their dad.

I ditched my first day of third grade with their son—he was four years older than me—and we went fishing instead, as if skipping school and casting a line would make us men. It seemed like fun, but it was really just rebellion dressed up in childhood curiosity.

That same year, I met a kid named Rob, or as I would come to call him, Rob Dogg. Even then, he had a street name. He lived just up the block and quickly became the ringleader of our little crew. We were kind of a neighborhood gang, though none of us would've called it that. To us, we were just kids being kids, running wild, chasing adrenaline, sneaking out, getting drunk, making trouble. In reality, we were boys with no guardrails and no boundaries.

We would often sneak wine from my dad's stash, pass it around like some rite of passage, then take off through the streets like we owned them. For a while, we were the kings of the neighborhood—or at least that's what it felt like. The truth was, we were lost boys looking for fathers, yearning for someone to say, "This is the way. Walk in it."

My older brother was no help. At that age, most little brothers idolize their big brothers, and I was no exception. He was caught in his own spiral of addiction and pain, and I followed close behind, mimicking his words, his habits, and his hollow bravado. He wound up dropping out of school and started spending more time with those same neighbors. And I, in turn, started shaping my identity around his broken example.

When we weren't getting into trouble in our own neighborhood, we would head out to my grandmother's house and cause trouble there. She had no idea what was going on. To her, we were just grandkids visiting for the weekend, but for us, it was another playground for our rebellion. With Grandma, we had more freedom, even less supervision, and another place to hide our growing darkness behind childhood smiles.

That's where I was introduced to pornography. We stumbled upon my uncle's collection of old magazines, and it was like we'd discovered a secret world. My brother egged me on, and I looked, and lingered. Pornography took root in my life right away. Yes, there had been earlier moments, brief and confusing encounters, like the time with the neighbor girl when I was even younger, but this was different. This was repeated, accessible, and unchecked, and it began to wrap itself around my soul like a vice.

Those years were about craving something real in a world that felt fake. I didn't know it then, but I was beginning to develop a deep soul wound that I would carry into adolescence, into manhood, even into ministry. A wound that would one day meet the healing power of grace.

But in third grade, I wasn't thinking about redemption. I was just a little boy trying to grow up too fast, chasing a dangerous freedom that promised everything and delivered nothing but pain and scars.

THE SEEDS AND THE CYCLE

By fourth grade, life had settled into a strange rhythm, if you could call it that. I was bouncing back and forth between my dad's house and my mom's. On the outside, it might've looked like I was just a kid adjusting to life after divorce, but on the inside, I was trying to grow up way too fast.

I was still just a child, but I had already crossed so many invisible lines that I barely remembered where they were supposed to be. It's hard to pinpoint the moment when I stopped being a boy and started carrying the burdens of a broken world on my shoulders. All I knew was that I didn't feel safe. Not in my dad's house, not in my mom's, and not in my own skin.

In all of this, there was no mention of God, Jesus, or faith, not in our day-to-day lives and not in the conversations around the dinner table. We didn't pray before meals or attend church on Sundays. We were too busy trying to survive.

The only exception was my grandmother. She was a Jehovah's Witness. That's not a faith tradition I would come to align with, but she was the only one who ever brought up the name of Jesus during those years. She would sit me down at her kitchen table in Burlington, open her Bible, and speak softly about things I didn't understand but somehow knew mattered.

"There's more to life than what you can see," she would tell me. "There's a God who made you. There's a purpose for your life."

I didn't know what to do with that information back then, but I listened. I asked questions, and she answered patiently and honestly. She planted small seeds of truth that would take years to sprout, but at least they were planted. I'm grateful for that.

Of course, not every memory was entirely pleasant. I still laugh now when I recall the time she took us to a Jehovah's Witness conference. We endured long hours with no music, no snacks, and enough stale air to scare me off ever joining that church. I was a fidgety kid, and sitting through that conference felt like a preview of eternity, but not the kind my grandma was trying to sell me on.

Those summer visits to Burlington were always a mixed bag. On one hand, there was my grandma's voice of quiet faith. On the other, there was also my uncle Randy, my dad's brother. He was the textbook "creepy uncle," the one every family seems to have but no one wants to talk about. A grown man in his thirties or forties, still living at home and acting like a teenager. He was a mess of drinking and drugs, and he had no problem providing me with alcohol, drugs, or pornography.

It was a cycle of behavior that came all too easy to me. Of course, I now believe it was a generational curse. These invisible chains get passed down in families from generation to generation. Cycles of addiction, abuse, poverty, rage, sexual sin. Nobody sits you down to explain how they work. They're just there, like the family heirloom nobody wants but everyone inherits. And they were alive and well in my family.

I watched these curses unfold in real time. The alcohol on my dad's side of the family had already claimed so many. I saw what it did to my brother. To my sisters. I saw how it seduced and destroyed people. How it promised comfort and delivered pain. It nearly took me out more than once, and eventually, it killed my dad, but we'll get to that later.

Of course, I couldn't possibly have known as a nine-year-old boy that I was repeating generational behavior patterns. I had no idea I was carrying around the generations of family sins like a backpack full of bricks.

And yet, even then, a few seeds had been planted. God's voice was whispering to me in the middle of all of that noise, offering a quiet hope that maybe, just maybe, there was a way out.

THE FIELD AND THE FURY

In the middle of the drinking, the drugs, the back-and-forth shuffle between houses, something unexpected and important showed up in my life: football.

Nobody pushed me into it. My mom didn't sign me up to keep me out of trouble. My dad didn't sit me down and say I needed structure. It was something *I* chose. Maybe for the first time in my young life, I looked around at the storm I was living in and decided I wanted something solid to hold onto, so I joined Little League.

Football quickly became my anchor. The practices gave me structure, and the games gave me purpose. More importantly, the coaches gave me expectations, and for a kid growing up in a world with no boundaries, that was a strange kind of gift. For those few hours each week, I wasn't a kid caught between two broken households. I wasn't the son of an alcoholic or the product of a generational curse. I was a player, a teammate, and as it turned out—I was pretty good.

I played both sides of the ball, every down, every play. No matter what team I was on, the coaches trusted me with key positions, and I loved it. I didn't realize it then, but that field became holy ground for me. It was a sacred space where I felt like I mattered, but even in those moments of light, the shadows followed.

My dad almost never came to my games. I didn't think much of it at the time, or at least, that's what I told myself. I learned early how to bury pain before I even had the words for it. But years later, I can still remember what it felt like to look up at the sideline and not see him there. The rare times he *did* show up, it felt like Christmas morning. I'd play harder, run faster, hoping he'd see me—*really* see me. I was trying to earn the kind of attention I craved but never got at home.

By middle school, I was playing for two teams at once: Little League and the school team. It was grueling, but I didn't care. I was hooked, and more than that, I was thriving.

However, back home, the old patterns were still running full speed. Going back and forth between my parents' homes only made the "dangerous freedom" worse. I knew I could get away with more at my mom's house, and I took full advantage of it. Every other weekend turned into a full-blown party of drinking, smoking, and sneaking out.

My mom had a boyfriend then, a guy named Greg, and he had a son, Robert. Robert was a year older than me, and we clicked right away. Every summer, he would stay with us for a month, and that month would be pure chaos. We would run wild, push boundaries, get high, and live like we had no consequences.

Then fifth grade came, and with it, another crack in the foundation.

My dad got his third DUI and went back to jail. That left us with Paula. She was never equipped to take care of anyone, least of all children. She was lost in her own addictions, and our house fell into darkness. Not just moral or spiritual darkness but *literal* darkness. She couldn't stay on top of the bills, and the power got shut off. I remember cold nights and empty cabinets, welfare boxes on the porch. My grandma would visit and try to help however she could, but there was only so much she could do.

Marissa was just a little girl, maybe six or seven. Rochelle was barely a toddler. And Paula, the woman left in charge, was spiraling. She was unpredictable at best, dangerous at worst. I've described her before as a loose cannon, but that doesn't quite capture the raw fear she could unleash.

One night, Paula took it to a frightening new level.

There was a party at the house—just another blur of people and noise. I don't remember what triggered it, but Paula got so mad at me that she attacked me. She cornered me in the bathroom and unleashed her rage. She slammed the door shut and laid into me, pinning me down and choking me, slapping me, punching me in the stomach, pinching my skin until it bruised, all while screaming at the top of her lungs.

The smell of alcohol on her breath was sharp and sour, and her voice didn't sound right. I remember it vividly, and it seemed as if a demon were speaking through her. The attack went on forever—at least an hour, maybe more.

I was just a kid, and no one came to help me. In fact, I don't remember how it ended. I don't remember who pulled her off me—if anyone did. It was all a haze of fear and pain followed by silence.

My brother wasn't there. My dad was in jail. My mom didn't know. And in that moment, I realized just how alone I really was.

That night never left me. Although I later forgave her—as a man of faith, I've had to walk the road of forgiveness many times—I never looked at her the same. I never called her "Mom." She was just Paula and always would be.

That was a very dark time in my life, but even then, I had football. Even then, I had those Friday night lights, those muddy fields, those times where I could run and hit and sweat and forget. For a little while, the noise in my head would go quiet.

I see now that God was using even something as simple as football to keep me breathing, to whisper, "I'm not done with you yet."

A LIGHT IN THE DARKNESS

My dad would get out of jail, and things would go back to "normal"—until the next DUI, the next disappearance, the next collapse. The cycle wasn't slowing down. If anything, it was gaining momentum.

Right in the middle of all that madness, God sent a ray of light into the darkness. That light was my fifth-grade teacher, Ms. Hanlan, who everyone called "Ms. H."

Ms. H was different from all the other adults in my life. She didn't look at me like I was damaged or hopeless. She understood the kind of life I was living, but she never let me use it as an excuse. She kept me in line, challenged me, and believed in me. When everything else was unstable, she became a pillar of consistency, the kind of adult I didn't even realize I needed.

One day, we were doing a class project on the human body. She came up to me and said, "Rick, I think *you* should present on the reproductive system."

I stared at her like she was insane. "Seriously?" I asked. "You want me to talk about penises and vaginas? In front of *everyone*?"

She nodded and smiled. "I think you can handle it."

It scared me to death, but she saw something in me I didn't see in myself. She saw a potential leader. That awkward classroom presentation, complete with giggling classmates and red-faced embarrassment, was my first taste of public speaking. It wouldn't be the last.

Isn't it funny how God uses strange things to prepare us for our calling?

Ms. H kept showing up in my story. Years later, when she left elementary school, she became principal of the alternative high school I attended. She saw the whole arc of my early life. The rise, the fall, the hurt, the hustle, and still, she never stopped believing in me.

The odds are stacked heavily against kids like me—children of addicts, victims of abuse, stuck in cycles of poverty and pain. The numbers aren't good. Generational curses don't break themselves. They chase you down, latch on, and try to drag you into the same darkness your parents fell into. If you don't know what you're fighting against, you won't stand a chance.

But Ms. H helped me fight. She gave me structure, accountability, and, maybe most importantly, a glimpse of what it looked like to *be* believed in. For a while, I held onto that. I even got to celebrate a rare moment of joy: sixth-grade continuation. Back then, sixth grade still counted as part of grade school, and "continuation" was like a mini graduation. My dad came. My grandma and grandpa were there too. I remember standing up tall, hearing my name called, walking across that little stage feeling like maybe, just maybe, things were going to be okay.

Summer was around the corner, and for the first time in a long time, I had hope. I was going into seventh grade. I had survived elementary school. I thought, *This is it. This summer's going to be the best one yet.*

But it wasn't. That summer everything changed.

I was spending the night at a friend's house when the phone rang. My mom was on the line. "I need to come get Rick," she told them. It wasn't her weekend. That alone seemed strange.

When she pulled up, I got into the car, confused and anxious. She looked at me, her face tight with worry, and said, "Your dad's been in a really bad car accident. He's in serious condition."

The breath left my body. All the hope I had been building suddenly collapsed. I buried my face into her lap and just wept. I didn't know how to process what she had just said. I had already lost my father in so many ways—to alcohol, jail, absence—but now I faced the possibility of losing him for good.

AFTER THE CRASH

Later that night, we found out the truth. Dad had been drinking again. He ran a stop sign and T-boned another car. The crash was brutal. It shattered his hip, broke his jaw, and punctured a lung. He bit off half his tongue. It was a miracle the other driver survived. It was a miracle *he* survived.

The fear of uncertainty returned, stronger than ever. Dad had just gotten out of jail not long before. He was the only one in the house bringing in money, and now he was broken physically, emotionally, and financially.

Looking back, I can say it plainly: My dad was a knucklehead. He was selfish and reckless, but I know now it wasn't just him. The demons of alcohol, addiction, and shame had a grip on him, and every time it seemed like he might be getting ahead, those demons dragged him back under.

After a few weeks in the hospital, they sent him home with a medical bed. His jaw was wired shut, so he was unable to speak clearly, and he was unable to move. My grandma moved in to help, but even with her there, things got so much worse. The power got shut off again as the money ran dry. We were out of options.

That's when my Aunt Flora stepped in. My dad's sister bailed us out financially, got the power turned back on, and did what she could to keep us afloat. Without her, I don't know what would've happened, but even as she tried to piece the external things back together, my dad was falling apart on the inside.

He was supposed to go to court, to face the consequences of the accident, but instead, he decided to run. Even though he was still healing from his injuries, he disappeared for months and stayed off the grid. He couldn't face what he had done. He never could.

Sadly, I learned the hard way the importance of having a strong father in the home. Kids need a dad who is present, who is sober, who is faithful and steady. That kind of man gives his kids a foundation to stand on. When a father leads with integrity, his children inherit stability, confidence, clarity, self-worth, and discipline, but when a father crumbles, everything crumbles with him.

I didn't get a strong, stable father, and I've lived the consequences. My experiences weren't unique. The statistics are clear. Children without strong, stable fathers have a higher risk of depression, anxiety, and delinquency.[1] They tend to have a weaker performance in school and lower self-esteem. I lived with all of these.

---

[1] Children's Hospital Los Angeles, "A Father's Impact on Child Development," All for Kids, accessed May 27, 2025, https://www.allforkids.org/news/blog/a-fathers-impact-on-child-development.

I didn't know how to make good decisions because I hadn't seen what good decisions looked like. I didn't have an example to follow. All I had was wreckage—literal and symbolic—that would leave scars I still carry.

We never really recovered from dad's accident. Things became more desperate, and the nights got longer. I ended up moving in with my grandma before I started seventh grade. I just needed out. He came back from his time on the run, but he was spiraling badly. He'd gotten deeper into drugs and alcohol. The man who once tried to build a family was now busy tearing down whatever pieces remained.

Finally, one night, it all boiled over. He called my grandma's house, drunk and slurring his words. He was angry, crying, and screaming. I couldn't even understand what he was trying to say. Then, without warning, he showed up at Grandma's house with my little sister Rochelle in tow. He kissed me, hugged me, said some things that didn't make sense. Then he got in his van and drove off.

Later, I found out he went back to his house and exploded—fighting everyone there. A party was happening, and something must've set him off. He started swinging, screaming, throwing people out, wrecking the house in a drunken rage. The cops came, and he was arrested again.

This time, it was serious. He had been on the run, and there was a warrant out for him. Once again, my dad was behind bars.

I wasn't angry at him for going back to jail. As with his previous stints, I felt relief. When my dad was in jail, at least I knew he was sober and safe. He was in his right mind, so when we visited him, I could look in his eyes and see the man he might've been if the addiction hadn't devoured him. He was clean and present, so even though he was locked up, I felt like he was actually *there*.

To me, that became normal, and that's the real tragedy. As a kid, I didn't know any different. I thought this was how families worked. I thought jail was just another part of fatherhood. I didn't understand the gravity of it then, but as I grew older, I saw how history was waiting to repeat itself in my life. The same curse that wrapped around my father's life like a noose was already reaching for my neck.

The truth is, if someone doesn't name the curse, intentionally break the pattern, and walk in a new direction, it will keep going—from father to son, from son to grandson, generation after generation, until someone stands up and says, "Enough."

NEW AND OLD WOUNDS

I thank God for my grandma.

When everything else in my life was falling apart, she opened her door and took me in as her own. In many ways, she became my mother *and* my father during that time. Unfortunately, I was still carrying the survival instincts I'd picked up from years of dysfunction. I had learned to keep secrets and smile while hiding pain. I would nod while plotting my next escape. I was only thirteen, just on the edge of adolescence, but I had already become a master of living a double life.

To my grandparents, I was the grandson who showed up to dinner, stayed out of trouble, maybe even cracked a few jokes, but behind the scenes, I was experimenting even more with drugs and alcohol. I was sneaking out, lying, stealing, and looking for trouble. My grandma didn't know. She couldn't have known. Though she did her best to give me a new start, I hadn't yet learned how to leave the past behind.

Around that time, Paula—still tangled in her own demons—came back and took Rochelle home. Marissa had stayed behind after the crash, but now both girls were back in the house that had once held all of us together and then broken us apart. What happened in that house while my dad was in prison is something I still don't fully know. My sisters, Rochelle and Marissa, won't talk about it to this day. They've disowned Paula completely. They don't call her "Mom." They call her Paula, just like I did.

Whenever I ask about that season of their lives, there's only silence, and that silence says more than words ever could. It haunts me. What they must've seen, what they must've felt, what they were forced to endure. I was just a kid myself, but I wanted to protect them. I wanted to help, but I couldn't. I could barely hold my own head above water.

And yet, by the grace of God, they made it. Both of them are married now, both are in the navy, and they're living lives that defy the odds stacked against us. I'm proud of them, more than they probably know. They found a way out, and I thank God for that.

Still, when I look back on those bruised, blurry years, there's a heaviness I carry. Even as I settled into my grandma's house and prepared to start middle school, I knew the story wasn't over. I still had unhealed wounds and demons to face.

Paula had a nephew named Philip, and like so many others in our orbit, he was already living in the depths of addiction and pain. He was a runaway, raised in a house of violence, passed from group home to group home. At one point, he even lived with us.

He wasn't just lost, he was dangerous. He didn't threaten me or scare me—nothing like that. No, far worse, he *influenced* me. He taught me how to steal more efficiently, how to lie more convincingly, how to push every limit until consequences disappeared in the rearview mirror. He introduced me to even more drinking, smoking, and darkness.

Philip was a mirror, but one I didn't want to look into, because he was everything I was becoming. At thirteen years old, I was sitting on the edge of a generational cliff, with one foot already dangling over the edge.

But God, in His mercy, hadn't let go of me yet.

CHAPTER FOUR

THE DOWNWARD SPIRAL

BY THE TIME SEVENTH GRADE STARTED, I WAS LIVING FULL-time with my grandmother. We weren't in the safest neighborhood, but at least my grandma gave me a roof over my head, warm meals, and love. She tried to keep me grounded, but I was already running.

I fell in with some older neighborhood kids, boys who had older brothers and easy access to alcohol. We would throw parties almost every night. I was just a thirteen-year-old middle schooler pretending to be a man, chasing rebellion like it was the only prize worth having.

Through it all, football remained my anchor. That field was one of the only places I felt any real sense of purpose. It was something I could count on, even as everything else slipped further and further away.

But darkness was gaining on me fast. One night, my brother and his friends sold a man a fake sheet of acid, took the cash, and bought cocaine. That night, they were all using in the back room at my mom's house while I hung out in the front. One of his friends came over and offered me a real hit of acid. I didn't even hesitate; I took it.

Fourteen years old, and I was tripping on LSD for the first time. To be honest, I liked it. I liked the high. Even more, I liked the way it helped me forget the parts of my life I couldn't fix. And I liked my brother's friends, too. They made me feel like I was one of them.

Back at school, I was smoking weed with friends during lunch or ditching class altogether. At home, I was stealing cash from my grandma's lockbox. She kept a stash in her room, and every time I reached in, I stole more, chipping away at her trust. I hate that I did that to her. She probably thought she was losing her mind, wondering how a few coins or a folded bill went missing from time to time, but it was always me.

Even so, she would get up every morning and cook me breakfast like I was her sweet, beloved grandson. She made pancakes, bacon, toast—real hearty breakfast. She was used to feeding a dozen mouths, so she'd pile the plate high even though I never ate it all. I didn't deserve any of this, but that's who she was: faithful, generous, and loving. Though I didn't deserve it, she loved me like a son.

She was so innocent and trusting that I even convinced her to let me drive her Cadillac to football practice. I told her I had a permit. I didn't—I was barely fourteen—but she believed me.

"Okay, honey," she said sweetly, handing me the keys.

And there I was, pulling up to practice like I had it all together, even though I was a wreck in slow motion.

NEW YEAR'S EVE 1999

Then came Kelly.

I'd liked her since sixth grade, but it was in seventh that we really started dating. She was my first real girlfriend, and I loved her the best way a broken kid knows how to love. She gave me something to live for and aspire to. I wanted to be the kind of guy she could be proud of, but I didn't want her to know just how messed up I really was. I kept secrets and wore masks. I lied by omission.

On New Year's Eve 1999, we were in her parents' camper, tucked away in their backyard, watching *Braveheart* of all things. The world was supposed to end that night. All the experts said Y2K was going to cause a great computer crash and global chaos, and I guess we figured if everything was ending, why not cross the next threshold? And so, that night, I lost my virginity.

I wish I could say it was beautiful, or that it meant something, but it wasn't what I expected. It was confusing and surreal, and within weeks, everything got even more real. Kelly got pregnant.

The day Kelly told me she was pregnant, I remember the weight of it, and the panic that followed. We had used protection, but later I found out that a so-called friend of mine had played a sick joke. He'd taken a needle and poked holes in one of the condoms, trying to be funny. I didn't know. Neither did she.

We were just kids. She came from a good family and had solid, successful parents who were nothing like mine. Still, we didn't dare tell them. Instead, her cousin helped arrange an abortion. Looking back now, with what I believe and how deeply I value the sanctity of life, it crushes me. I carry that day like a scar on my soul.

We were scared. We didn't know what else to do. So we ended the life of our child before they had a chance to take a breath. It's one of my greatest regrets. The memory of that day has stayed with me. Until now, I've never told anyone that part of my story. Not my parents. Not even my closest friends. I've carried the guilt like a stone in my chest, and the truth is, I still do. But I also carry hope that one day, when I step into Heaven, I'll see the face of the child I never met: a life lost too soon, a life that's now in God's hands. I believe this because I've encountered the mercy of God in places I didn't think grace could reach.

STICKS, STONES, AND STUPID

Seventh and eighth grade were some of the darkest years of my life, not just because of the drugs and the parties or the secrets I carried, but because of something much smaller: a word.

There were a few teachers who saw through my brokenness and chose to pour into me. They knew what I was walking through, and they noticed when I showed up high to class or disappeared after first period. They knew I was running with the wrong crowd, getting suspended, fighting, skipping school to smoke weed behind the dumpsters. Some of them showed grace and tried to redirect me.

Other teachers were not so compassionate. I still remember walking into the gym one day, shoulders slumped, head down, just trying to get through the day. One of the teachers—I've forgotten his name, but not his face—looked at me with a sneer and said, "What are you doing in here, stupid?"

Just like that, sharp and loud, in front of everyone.

I froze. I don't even remember what I said in response. I mumbled something and walked away like it didn't matter, but it hurt me deeply for reasons I didn't even fully understand.

One of the greatest lies ever taught to a child is, "Sticks and stones may break my bones, but words will never hurt me."

This couldn't be further from the truth. Words *do* hurt, sometimes more than broken bones. They settle deep into our identity and quietly grow roots. That one word—*stupid*—became a seed that the enemy watered in my mind for years. I started saying it to myself and started believing it. Once I believed it, I started living like it.

You're just stupid. Don't speak up. You'll sound dumb. Don't try—what's the point?

By the time I felt God calling me into ministry, that word was still in the room with me. I would lie to avoid public speaking. I would dodge opportunities to lead. I would freeze in front of people because I was afraid they might see through me. I wasn't scared of preaching. I was scared of *looking stupid*.

That word didn't just shape my middle school years. It nearly stunted my calling. But right in the middle of all that noise and shame, something surprising happened. My dad—who had spent most of my life running from responsibility and drowning in addiction—started writing me letters from prison, and for the first time, he was talking about Jesus.

LETTERS FROM LOCKUP

When my dad went down for what was probably his seventh or eighth DUI, the judge had no more patience left. This time, he went to prison. He got two years in the Department of Corrections. No ankle monitor, no halfway house—just cold concrete, steel bars, and plenty of time to think about his mistakes.

That's when he started writing me letters, and they weren't like the ones he'd sent before, full of empty promises or complaints. These letters were about *Jesus*.

At first, I wasn't sure what to make of it. My dad talking about God? Talking about faith and forgiveness? My dad had never spoken about God, let alone *written* about Him. But now, from behind bars, he was telling me about his newfound faith. He claimed that Jesus had found him, and he was now reading the Bible. He believed he was being changed.

It felt almost fake, like maybe it was just another act he was putting on to get through his sentence, but then I visited him. He looked different. He was healthier, clear-eyed. This was no longer the angry, damaged man I'd known for most of my life. He was calm—even hopeful.

Honestly, I didn't know what to do with that. The same man who had wrecked so much of our family was now talking to me about grace and redemption? I didn't know it yet, but those letters, along with the quiet grace of my grandma, were shaping me. God was moving even in the mess. There was the voice that once called me *stupid*, but another Voice was beginning to whisper something new:

You are called. You are mine. You are not the names they gave you.

Dad missed all of my seventh- and eighth-grade years, but he told me about his plans for when he got out. He wanted to start a painting business, take us all to church, turn the page on everything we'd been through.

"I'm going to get it right this time," he said. "I want to get us back together and start fresh."

He didn't know what was going on back home with Paula, and I didn't tell him everything. I shared bits and pieces. For example, I told him how his sister, Auntie Flora, had been fighting tooth and nail to save the house from falling apart. How she'd stepped in when he tried to buy it before prison, putting it in his name and then waging war to get Paula out. There was drama between the two of them I didn't fully understand at the time, but at least I knew someone was finally trying to fight *for* us instead of *against* us.

For the first time in a long time, I felt something that almost resembled hope.

SHADOWS IN THE HOUSE

Still, even with my dad gone and my grandma doing her best to give me a stable home, there were still shadows in her house. My creepy Uncle Randy lived with us, and he was still a mess of drinking, drugging, no direction, and no restraint. Unfortunately, I started to lean on him like an older brother.

He'd buy us alcohol and hand it off like it was nothing. We would drink together, smoke weed together, swap lies, and escape from reality. He still had that endless stash of old porn magazines, and I would sneak into his room when he wasn't around, flipping through them like they held the answers to important questions.

That summer between seventh and eighth grade was when my addiction to pornography deepened. It wasn't curiosity anymore. It was consumption and comfort—a counterfeit kind of intimacy in a world where real love often came with pain or abandonment.

And then came another blow. My grandma, the rock of our fractured family, the one person still standing strong in the storm, was diagnosed with colon cancer. She was the one holding it all together. She had opened her door to me, fed me, prayed for me, and loved me, even as I stole from her and snuck around behind her back. Now *she* was sick, and it was serious.

Chemo started. Family came and went. Her strength began to fade. Through it all, I just kept spiraling. I was a teenager lost in addiction, grief, confusion, and still trying to pretend I had control. Uncle Randy was off doing his own thing, and I was doing mine. No one really knew how to help.

That was the summer the foundation cracked for good. The woman who had become a mother to me was fighting for her life, and I didn't know how to process that kind of loss.

I look back on that season and I see a teenager walking through fire with no map, no guide, just a stack of letters from a father in prison talking about a Savior I hadn't yet come to know. Somehow, even then, God was planting seeds. In prison cells, in hospital rooms, in quiet bedrooms full of grief and guilt, God was there, even when I didn't know how to call on His name.

That summer, Grandma's house smelled like spray paint. We weren't painting anything, but Uncle Randy had started huffing. He would sneak off to the basement with rattle cans, and the chemical stink of it would waft through the vents and taint the air. Meanwhile, just one floor above him, my grandma was fighting for her life. She was frail, hair thinning, her bones aching from chemo.

The contrast was unbearable, and one day, I snapped. I marched downstairs to confront Uncle Randy, and we got into it. Shouting turned to shoving. Shoving turned to fists. Eventually, I called the cops. When they came and dragged him out, I thought, *Finally, some peace for Grandma. Some dignity in her own house.*

But deep down, I knew I was no better. While Randy was downstairs huffing paint, I was in the back room lighting up weed. I had judgment in one hand and a blunt in the other. My life had become a double helix of contradiction between sin and sincerity, rebellion and remorse, all of it tangled so tightly that I could barely tell where one version of me ended and the other began.

At school, I was a ghost in the system—barely showing up, barely passing. The only reason I got through eighth grade was because Kelly practically carried me across the finish line. She did my book reports and helped me study. She believed in me more than I believed in myself. I still remember thinking, *She deserves better*, but I wasn't ready to admit how deep I was falling or how far I'd strayed.

Kelly knew about the drinking and the weed, but she didn't know the rest. Not the LSD or the stealing. Not the pornography. I kept that stuff in the shadows, out of her reach. I loved her, but I didn't know how to be *whole* with her. I was trying to be two different people—one for her, one for everyone else—and somewhere in the middle, I was losing myself.

At the same time, my dad kept writing to me from prison, letter after letter, each one filled with the name I wasn't used to hearing him say: *Jesus*. He told me he was clean, that God had done something real in him, and I started to believe him. It was the most sober and the most *alive* I had ever seen him.

And then, at the end of eighth grade, he came home. He got the house back. Paula was gone. My siblings and I moved back in. Dad followed through—he launched that painting business and got us to church. And somehow, in that fragile but beautiful season, I gave my heart to Christ.

That summer was a turning point. I was one of those sudden transformation stories. I stopped hanging out with my old crew, dumped my stash, and stopped listening to the music that fed my flesh. I was the kid who suddenly started quoting Scripture and talking about Jesus—a full-on Bible thumper, and I loved it.

It was freedom and not the *dangerous* kind I had lived in before, but a holy kind—filled with conviction and peace. For the first time, I wasn't looking for a way to numb the pain. I was chasing purpose.

Even my brother sobered up and accepted Christ. It felt like we were given a second chance—me, my dad, my brother. Three broken men trying to rebuild a home with Jesus at the center. There were no parties in the house that summer. No Paula, no Randy. Just early mornings, family dinners, and Sunday services. I wanted nothing more than to stay in that light forever.

But darkness doesn't give up so easily. My mom's house was still a revolving door of compromise. By then, she'd stopped even pretending to disapprove of my self-destructive behavior. She let me drink and smoke around her. It was easier that way for both of us. While I was trying to live out my faith, every other weekend dragged me back into the old world and the old me.

CHAPTER FIVE

THROWING IN THE TOWEL

I STILL CAN'T FULLY EXPLAIN HOW RADICAL THE CHANGE was in my life. It was a complete shift, as if God reached into the middle of my mess and turned the light on. One moment I was chasing everything the world had to offer—drugs, pornography, money—and the next, I was hungry for something holy.

Before we get into this, I want to encourage you to keep following me on this journey. If you're not a Christian, you might be a little turned off by all the Jesus talk, and that's okay. I was too, at one point in my life. Then again, you might find something here that speaks to you in ways you don't expect.

You see, it was as if my soul woke up. I remember sitting on the edge of my bed with my CD binder—the kind every kid had back then. The thick, leather-bound binder was filled with discs of every genre: rap, rock, grunge, club anthems, all of it. Without overthinking it, I tossed them all in the trash one by one. I didn't need them anymore. I didn't *want* them. It wasn't that someone told me to do it. I just knew that if I was serious about following Jesus, something had to go, so I let it go.

I cut ties with all the guys I used to run with—Rob Dogg and the rest of the neighborhood crew. There were about nine of us, and we were thick as thieves. But when Jesus grabbed hold of me, I couldn't do both. I couldn't follow Him while holding onto the crowd that had pulled me into darkness.

I chose Jesus, and for a brief moment, it felt like everything in life fell into place in a beautiful way. Life with my dad felt stable. The more he worked in his painting business, the more it felt like we were becoming normal. We were a real family who went to church together and ate meals at the kitchen table. I went to youth group every week and started telling *everybody* about Jesus—my mom, her boyfriend, even strangers. I couldn't help it. My transformation was loud and full of light.

At that time, I was attending a youth group at a church called Centerpoint Christian Outreach Center. My dad had found a home church of his own—Crossroads Church of Denver, pastored by Tom Stipe. Somewhere between those two places, God started speaking to me in ways I had never experienced before.

I'll never forget one night at youth group. The music was playing, and I was standing in the middle of worship when it felt like the finger of God touched the top of my head. I don't have any other way to describe it. Just a presence. Electricity. It surged from the crown of my head down to the soles of my feet, and I collapsed onto the bleachers, sobbing uncontrollably.

I know now it was the baptism of the Holy Spirit, but at the time, I didn't have language for it. I didn't grow up in a house where we talked about the things of God. Nobody coached me into this moment. It just *happened*, and it made me hungry for more—more of God, more of His Word, more of whatever healing and peace He could give.

Lord knows, I had trauma that needed healing. I was carrying more than a decade's worth of pain and dysfunction, not to mention father wounds, addiction, and shame. It didn't all disappear overnight, but it started to come to the surface. I began to realize that following Jesus wasn't just about saying a prayer or changing your music. It was about letting Him peel back the layers of your soul and touch the wounded places no one else could reach.

That summer, it felt like everything was beginning again. Like the first pages of a new chapter. Hope was no longer a far-off fantasy, but something I could actually feel. My dad was sober, I was saved, my brother was clean, and Paula was gone.

For the first time in my life, I dared to believe the peace might last.

TWO VOICES

There was a night in my bedroom I'll never forget. I was fifteen years old. Worship music played softly in my ears through a pair of cheap headphones as I sat on the edge of my bed, lost in the presence of God. It was one of those moments that felt sacred, peaceful. I loved worship. It always quieted the chaos in me.

Suddenly, that peace was interrupted. I heard two distinct voices. Not out loud—not in the way you hear a person speak across a room—but in that still, unmistakable way the soul knows something is being said. It reminded me of the old Bugs Bunny cartoons—the angel on one shoulder, the devil on the other, whispering competing advice. Only this time, it felt real.

The first voice was calm and clear. *"Rick, you're not supposed to be with the girl you're dating. You need to break up with her."*

Then came the second voice. It was sharper and darker. *"What are you doing with your life? Haven't you lived yet?"*

In an instant, I was caught in between. I didn't want to break up with Kelly. She was my high school sweetheart, and we'd been through so much together. But the second voice pulled at something deeper. It reminded me of all the things I had walked away from when I gave my life to Christ. The friends, the parties, the recklessness. It spoke with the seduction of freedom, as if I'd missed out on something the first time around.

That weekend, I went to church like usual. Centerpoint

Church was a lively, charismatic church where altar calls were common. Pastor Mark Ramsey was preaching. When he invited people forward for prayer, I felt the tug to respond. I went forward, and the pastor laid his hand on me. He began to speak prophetically—words that pierced right through me.

"You have a pastoral call on your life," he said.

A flood of emotion rose up in me—not awe or joy, but fear. Deep, paralyzing fear. Remember, I was fifteen years old. In my mind, being a pastor meant standing in front of people, opening your mouth, and being exposed. I flashed back to fifth grade, to Ms. Hanlan's class, when I was forced to give that embarrassing anatomy presentation in front of the whole room. I flashed back to the teacher in seventh grade calling me stupid. I still carried the embarrassment of both incidents, and now I was supposed to feel those same feelings every week for the rest of my life?

No, thank you.

I began to believe the second voice.

You're too young for this. You haven't lived. Why give it all up now?

Just like that, I turned my back on God. It wasn't some dramatic rebellion, but a quiet, fear-driven decision. A whisper in my heart that said, *"I'll come back later, but right now, I'm going to live my life."*

What did that look like? It started with the music. The CDs I had thrown away came back. I bought new ones. I started smoking weed again, only now I had to hide it. I didn't want my dad or my brother to know. I still went to church and sat through the sermons. I played the part, but inside, I was somewhere else entirely.

Then one afternoon I pulled into a gas station. I had just turned sixteen. I was filling up when a familiar face pulled up beside me: Rob Dogg. It had been a while since I'd seen him. We started talking and catching up. It didn't take long before the invitation came.

"You should come hang out again."

So I did. Just like that, I was back in the mix, hanging with the crew, the drugs, the alcohol, the women. Only this time it was deeper, darker, and a lot more intense. The stakes were higher now, and I wasn't just dabbling in temptation anymore. I was choosing it.

I had heard God's call. I had felt His presence. I had seen what life could look like with Him. But in that moment, I didn't want it.

There's a passage in Scripture that haunted me for years before I understood it fully. It's found in Matthew 12:43–45:

> When the unclean spirit has gone out of a person, it passes through waterless places seeking rest, but finds none. Then it says, "I will return to my house from which I came." And when it comes, it finds the house empty, swept, and put in order. Then it goes and brings with it seven other spirits more evil than itself, and they enter and dwell there. And the last state of that person is worse than the first.

I *lived* that verse.

I had been clean. I got saved. I had experienced the presence of God. I'd thrown away my music, walked away from my old friends, filled my life with Scripture and worship. I was a different person. But when I chose to walk away from God, the darkness came back sevenfold. And when it came, it brought more than just temptation—it brought destruction.

At sixteen, I was free-falling, and I dove straight into the drug trade like I had something to prove. My friends and I were barely old enough to drive, and we thought we were untouchable. We started small, flipping ounces. Then pounds. Then kilos. By the time we were seventeen, we were trafficking serious weight, acting like we were cartel bosses in a high school hallway.

Strip clubs welcomed us with open arms. Bouncers knew our

names. We had fake IDs, pockets full of cash, and women every night who didn't know or didn't care how young we really were.

I thought I had arrived, but behind the swagger was a soul that was crumbling. I was still living under my dad's roof. This man who had finally gotten clean, who had started going to church, who believed in me again. While he was building a life of restoration, I had a *kilo of cocaine* hidden in my bedroom.

The memory of that makes me physically ill. I think about my dad walking by my door. I think about what might've happened if he had opened the wrong drawer, or if law enforcement had shown up at the house. I was reckless, arrogant, and blinded by sin.

I wasn't just dealing—I was using heavily. One of the unspoken rules of drug dealing is that you don't dip into your own supply, but I did. I dipped into it over and over. The very thing I was selling to others became my personal escape hatch. It started with weed. Then ecstasy. Then cocaine. Then meth. And the further I went, the harder it was to stop.

Football was the only thread left holding me to any sort of stability. It was the only reason I still showed up to school, though barely. I was failing most of my classes, sleeping through the few I actually attended, but I kept showing up for practice. Those few hours in the dirt and sweat gave me just enough structure to fool myself into thinking I hadn't lost everything, but I had.

One day, I was skipping school again over at my buddy Eric's house. We'd been smoking meth for two, maybe three hours straight. I was deep in it, riding the high, when my phone started ringing. It was my dad.

I ignored it. Then it rang again. Then again. On the third call, he left a voicemail. My hands were shaking when I hit play.

"Rick, your grandma passed away."

I sat there frozen, my brain trying to break through the fog of chemicals and adrenaline and denial. My grandma was the one person who had been a constant source of love in my life. The one who had cooked me breakfast when I didn't deserve it. Who had taken me in. Prayed for me. Protected me. She was gone.

I didn't move. I didn't go home. I didn't even cry. No, I stayed right there, and I kept smoking meth.

That moment became a scar in my soul. The realization that I could be so lost, so consumed with myself and my sin, that I couldn't even stop to grieve the woman who had carried me when no one else would. She was the matriarch of our family, and my safety net, and I let her go without even standing up.

That was the consequence of letting my soul remain "swept and put in order" but *empty*. When I walked away from God, I left the door wide open, and seven more demons walked right in. Now, they had almost complete control over me.

LOSING THE ANCHOR

When my grandma passed away, the family didn't fall apart overnight. There wasn't some dramatic explosion or visible collapse, but something sacred was gone. With her death, I lost the one place that had always been safe. Her house was where I could always go to rest, to be fed, prayed for, and forgiven. Without her, there was no more center, no more steady ground.

She was remarkable. That woman who raised twelve children and still had enough room in her heart and her home for a small army of grandkids. At her funeral, they read aloud the numbers: thirty-three grandchildren, forty-four great-grandchildren to count, and a legacy that felt larger than life. I stood there, a troubled teenager with a heart full of regret. I had stolen from her, lied to her, disrespected her while she cooked me breakfast and gave me a bed. But even so, she loved me.

Even as a Jehovah's Witness, she planted the first seeds of belief in me. She told me about Jesus. She was the first person to give me a vocabulary for the spiritual, and those early seeds eventually took root. I believe that I am where I am today, in part, because of her faithfulness.

Losing her pushed me deeper into the spiral.

Ninth grade came and went in a blur. I didn't have a good experience in school, mostly because I was never really *in* school. I ditched constantly and failed to connect with the other students. The teachers didn't get me, and I didn't care. I was known as one of the worst kids in the building. I'd mouth off to teachers or curse them out in front of the class. Sometimes, I walked out of class without permission. I even got into fights in the middle of lectures.

It's ironic—God's sense of humor, maybe—that today, I'm married to a schoolteacher. My wife earned a master's degree in science and education. She spent our first seven years of marriage teaching high school, and now she's a middle school dean. Some nights she comes home venting about a student who cussed her out or stormed out of class, and I'll just sit there, quietly remembering the kid I used to be.

I wasn't a bad kid for the sake of being bad. I was broken, and I didn't know how to cope. I had developed this attitude that said, *"F___ it. I'm going to do what I want, and nobody's going to stop me. I don't need anyone. I'll figure it out on my own."*

That mindset came from growing up with a father who was in and out of my life—here one day, gone the next. I never knew when he would disappear again. I never knew which version of him I was going to get, so I learned to take care of myself. I learned to stop depending and forge my own path. I told myself I didn't need a dad. I didn't need anyone. That became my armor.

So as tenth grade began, I was still deeply tangled in the mess—still partying, still sneaking out, still pretending to follow Jesus while quietly rejecting Him. I was still with the girl I knew I wasn't supposed to be with. I was still hiding drugs, hiding sin, hiding from the truth.

At least I had football. That summer, we started two-a-days, and I was excited. Something inside of me whispered, *If I can turn it around on the field, maybe I can turn it around in the classroom too.* There was a flicker of hope. A tiny spark. Like maybe, just maybe, the story didn't have to end in darkness.

WHEN THE THREAD SNAPPED

Tenth grade was supposed to be my turning point. Football was back, school was starting, and I thought maybe things could change.

A handful of us had played Little League together, marched through middle school side by side, survived the wild mess of ninth grade, and now here we were. Sophomores with our shoulder pads on and our helmets in hand. We were the future of the varsity squad, and the coaches knew it. We had chemistry, camaraderie, and talent. We were the team to watch, and I was ready.

Then came that fateful Thursday. It was the last practice before our first game. We were wrapping up drills when the coach walked over. His face was tight, serious. He pulled me aside.

"Scadden, I've got some bad news."

I didn't expect what came next.

"You can't play tomorrow."

"What? Why?"

He looked down at the clipboard in his hand, like it could somehow soften the blow. "Your grades," he said. "They're too low. They've carried over from last year. You're failing most of your classes. I just can't let you play."

At that moment, a wave of crushing disappointment hit me. It knocked the air out of me, but it didn't take long for the old anger to rise up again. That same inner voice I'd been listening to for years whispered, *"F___ it. Who cares? Do what you want. No one's coming to save you."*

So I turned my back on the coach, walked off the field, and

never looked back. That was the exact moment the last thread in my life snapped.

Football had been my anchor. It was the last thing keeping me tethered to any sense of normalcy. Even when school was a disaster, even when my home life was unpredictable, football was *mine*, and now, that was gone too.

I walked into the locker room, peeled off my gear, got dressed, and left school that day. I never went back.

When I got home, I told my dad flat out, "I'm dropping out of school. I'm done."

He looked at me for a long moment, then said, "If you're not going to school, you're going to work."

I nodded. "Okay. I'm good with that."

And that was it. No arguments. No pleading. He hired me into his painting business, but I couldn't even hold that together. My nights became longer and darker. The parties got wilder. The drug trafficking got heavier. My friends and I were staying out until dawn, chasing highs. I'd come home reeking of liquor and bad decisions. My dad would try to rouse me for work, but I was either hungover or still buzzing. I missed jobs. I missed payments.

My addiction was swallowing me whole.

That Thursday on the football field, I lost a version of myself that still had a chance. I lost the hopeful version that still believed there might be more. Once that person was gone, I gave myself fully to the lie I had already started to believe: *This is who you are. This is all you'll ever be.*

THE DRUG I COULDN'T SHAKE

By the time I was deep into crack cocaine, everything else in my life had blurred. I'd tried a lot of drugs by then—weed, pills, acid, meth—but crack was different. It wasn't just another high. It was a choke hold, something primal that wrapped itself around me and wouldn't let go.

I was scared of it. This was the one addiction I actually feared because no matter how many times I told myself, *This is the last hit*, I kept going back. I was slipping faster than I could climb, and the terrifying part was I didn't know how to stop. I didn't even know *if* I could stop.

While I was descending into that pit, I was still trying to hold onto someone who no longer fit in the world I was creating. Kelly was still my girlfriend, but the gap between who we were was growing wider by the day.

She was a good girl. Brilliant and focused, she had a 4.0 GPA and was thriving in school. Kelly had a future. She had dreams and a clear direction, and then there was me—always chasing the next high, waking up hungover with no plan beyond the next night's party.

The relationship had become a slow, painful collapse. There were moments we would cling to each other like it was still the beginning, but deep down, we both knew it was breaking.

I didn't make it any easier. As the relationship slowly fell apart, I became jealous and controlling. I wouldn't call it stalking, but I would drive by to "check in" on her, see where she was, who she was with. Every glance she gave another guy felt like betrayal. Every laugh she shared with someone else felt like a wound. I wanted her to love me the way she used to, even though I was no longer the guy she fell for. I was trying to live two lives again—clinging to her light while plunging deeper into the shadows—but the darkness always wins when you try to live divided.

The drugs were winning, our relationship was losing, and I was stuck somewhere in the middle, pretending I could keep both. But deep down, I knew I was losing them both.

CHAPTER SIX

ANGELS AND DEMONS

LOOKING BACK, I CAN'T IMAGINE LETTING MY OWN KID drop out of school. I just wouldn't allow it. Yet, that's exactly what happened in my own life. It seems crazy now, but at the time, it felt like something I had to do to survive. Now that I'm walking in my calling, living the purpose God set for me, I understand why everything tried so hard to pull me off course. The enemy knew. He knew what was coming. That's why he tried to derail me early, and often. At no time was that more obvious than during one of the lowest and most chaotic chapters of my life.

Even now, I can still see that day like it's unfolding right in front of me. I had Kelly's truck. She'd loaned it to me to run a quick errand, just to the store and back, but instead of doing what I said I would, I called up Rob Dogg, my old running partner, and we headed to a strip club. It was midday. We had no plan—just impulse and poor judgment fueled by alcohol and pride.

We walked in with pockets full of cash, and the dancers flocked to us like bees to sugar. We were loud, reckless, drunk, and attracting the wrong kind of attention. There were some guys there who didn't appreciate the scene we were making. Tensions grew, but we didn't care.

Eventually, we went to leave, only to realize the truck keys were missing. I couldn't find them anywhere. I assumed I'd locked them inside, so I did what made sense in my twisted state of mind: I smashed out the back window. But when we checked inside the truck, there were still no keys.

It turns out, someone had found them and turned them in at the bar. I'd broken the window for nothing.

I got the keys and returned to the truck only to find those same guys from earlier waiting for us outside. One walked up to Rob Dogg, the other to my side of the truck. There were no words exchanged, just a sucker punch straight to my face.

Dazed and furious, I jumped behind the wheel and peeled out of there, barely able to see straight. I managed to pull into a grocery store parking lot, completely hammered. I couldn't drive anymore. That's when her dad started blowing up my phone. Kelly was looking for me. She wanted her truck back, and her dad wanted answers.

I looked at Rob Dogg and said, "Man, I can't do this anymore. You're going to have to walk." He got out and started walking, and I passed out right there on the curb.

The next thing I remember is Kelly's dad slapping me in the face, trying to wake me up. He loaded me into the truck, screaming the whole way home. I had a black eye, her truck had a busted-out window, and I was still completely wasted.

He dropped me off at my dad's house, and then all hell broke loose. My dad came in, furious after hearing what happened. Instead of shrinking back or apologizing, I exploded. Years of anger, pain, and shame came pouring out. I started yelling, cussing him out, blaming him for everything.

Then he hit me. Not a slap or a shove but a full-blown punch that sent me flying across the room. I hit the ground hard, and before I could fully process it, he was upstairs calling the cops.

I snapped. I started tearing my room apart, ripped the door off the hinges, punched holes in the drywall. I threw furniture. It wasn't just rage. It was grief, fear, trauma, and years of silence erupting all at once.

When the police arrived, I was crouched in a corner. I could hear them talking, trying to get me to respond, but panic had taken over. That's when I remembered I had an ounce of meth in my pocket.

I went cold. In that moment, survival mode kicked in. I didn't think—I just acted. I stripped off all my clothes and threw them in the corner, hoping the cops wouldn't check them when they arrested me. It was irrational. It was desperate. But somehow, it worked. They grabbed a different set of clothes, and I made it through the search without getting caught.

Somehow, again, I slipped by. I wouldn't call it luck. It was more like God's protection, even when I didn't deserve it. But the night wasn't over. When I told the officers I didn't want to live anymore, they took me seriously. They drove me to the hospital, where I was evaluated and eventually transferred to a youth psychiatric facility.

I spent three days there under observation. I met with counselors and got prescribed antidepressants. It was surreal. The truth is I was drowning, but I was too proud to say, "Help."

The meds didn't fix anything. They only made me feel numb and even more disconnected. When I got out, I told my dad I wanted to go back to school. He agreed and enrolled me in an alternative high school. It was a short stint—just a few months—but it was the first flicker of hope I'd seen in a long stretch of darkness.

Honestly, that whole season of my life was a war. I was at war with my father, with Kelly's family, with the police, but more importantly, I was in a spiritual battle for my soul. That battle had been raging for years, and the devil was playing for keeps. He threw everything he had at me in those days, but God wasn't done.

He never is.

Even in that strip club, even in that hospital bed, even in the corner of that torn-up bedroom, His grace was there. His protection was active, and somewhere beneath the wreckage of addiction and rebellion, the calling was still alive. I just hadn't answered it yet.

TRIPPING FOREVER

My first day at the alternative high school, I had a shock. The principal of the school was Ms. Hanlen. She had been my fifth- and sixth-grade teacher, the same one who had seen something in me. She'd poured into me back then with a sense of hope, even when I couldn't see it myself. And now, here she was again.

She was older and wiser, and she was now working with a school full of kids society had all but given up on. I was one of them. I was nearly seventeen, underweight, strung out, and angry. The hope I'd carried into that school was faint, like a flicker in the wind, but Ms. Hanlen knew my history. She saw more than the clothes or the attitude. She knew what I'd come from, and she saw what I was becoming.

I wish I could say I rose to the occasion. I didn't.

Alternative high schools are full of kids like me—smart but wounded, streetwise but lost. It didn't take long for me to find the ones who still wanted to party, still wanted to chase highs and hide from pain. We understood each other too well. That bond is magnetic when you're broken.

One night, I went home with two guys I met at school. We smoked weed together. That was nothing unusual for me at the time, but something was off. This wasn't normal weed. I still don't know what it was laced with, but I felt it hit hard and fast. My heart began to pound like it was trying to escape my chest. Panic set in, a rising terror that overwhelmed me.

I also had the antidepressants I'd been prescribed after my

hospital stay coursing through my veins, and whatever was in that weed didn't mix well. It triggered a deep sense of horror in my body and mind. I went home in that state, desperate and terrified. I called the treatment center that had given me the pills, begging for answers or some kind of direction, but they offered nothing.

I quit my meds cold turkey, but the damage was done. To this day, my body hasn't fully recovered from that bad trip. I still live with visual distortions; my peripheral vision flashes randomly, like a glitch that won't resolve. It's subtle, but constant, a scar left behind from that night.

Even so, not long after, I found myself back with Rob Dogg, chasing another high. This time, it was acid. We each took two and a half hits, enough to blast us straight out of reality. We were tripping hard, laughing, wandering, and staring at the sky like it held all the answers.

Then the sun started to rise. The trip hadn't ended, and I had to go home.

Still high, I managed to slip into the house. My dad left for work, and I lied and told him I was going to school. Instead, I went to a friend's house to wait it out.

That's where everything fell apart again. We were sitting there in silence when he said something that landed like an atomic bomb in my brain: "What if you trip forever?"

To someone sober, it's a strange, stoner thought, but to someone mid-trip, it's a profoundly frightening possibility. Once again, my mind collapsed into anxiety. My heart began racing, and that familiar, unwelcome panic returned, stronger than ever. I ran home, certain I was dying. I started praying—out loud, desperate.

"God, please...please don't let me trip forever."

I remember lying in bed, begging for clarity, for normalcy. I couldn't control my mind, couldn't ground myself. The fear felt physical, like drowning from the inside out.

And then, after hours of fighting through it, something

changed. Peace washed over me, not all at once, but enough to feel the panic lift. Enough to feel God's presence. I didn't know it then, but that was grace showing up again.

Sadly, my time at the alternative high school didn't last long. It was only a couple of months. One day, I told my dad I was done for good—no more school. I just wanted to work. He let it happen, and that was that.

I was done with school for good, but the drugs weren't done with me.

I wasted so many opportunities back then. I wasted my potential, I neglected relationships, but still, God didn't give up on me. His presence didn't disappear because I ran. I wish I'd applied myself more in school. I wish I'd listened, but more than that, I'm grateful that God never stopped chasing me.

SLICK RICK'S DARKEST MOMENT

I wish someone had stopped me. I wish my football coach had chased me down when I walked off that field and said, "Don't quit. Let's do this together." I wish one of my parents had drawn a line in the sand and said, "No, you're not dropping out of school. You're not giving up." But no one did. So I did what I wanted, and I paid for it.

The truth is, I didn't have a good model for what it looked like to make wise decisions. My dad made terrible decisions consistently. He taught me how to look out for myself, not how to lead myself, so when it came time to take control of my life, I followed in his footsteps and fell just as hard.

It's strange how life hinges on seemingly small decisions. You don't always realize in the moment how a fork in the road will define you. I wonder what would've happened if I'd stayed in football. If I hadn't turned my back on God. If I'd broken up with Kelly sooner or stayed with her longer.

Eventually, my father decided he'd had enough of my self

destruction. My drug use had escalated, and I had zero respect for his house, his rules, or him. I was seventeen when he looked me in the eye and said, "You've got to go."

"Where am I supposed to go?" I asked.

"That's not my problem," he replied.

As hard as it was to hear, I think he did the right thing.

I started calling around, trying to find a place to land. One of my contacts, an older woman I knew, offered a solution. "Move in with me," she said. "We'll split the rent."

So that's what I did. At seventeen years old, I was living on my own, flush with drug money, and had no one to answer to. It was the beginning of one of the darkest chapters of my life. Imagine a teenager with cash, connections, a steady supply, no curfew—and no accountability. My life became a party that never ended.

My friends and I used to joke that we were living like the guys in *Goodfellas*, driving around in tricked-out cars, music blasting, drugs in the trunk, money in our pockets, and power on our minds. I was the only white guy in the crew, so they called me *Güero*. My nickname on the streets was Slick Rick, and I wore that name like a crown.

In reality, there's no such thing as a never-ending party. After about eight months of wild living, I came home to find an eviction notice taped to our door. It turns out my roommate hadn't been paying the rent. She'd been taking my money and blowing it—on what, I never found out, but it didn't matter. I was out on the street again.

With nowhere else to go, I moved in with my mom. That was one of the biggest mistakes I ever made.

Mom had her own demons. Her boyfriend Greg was a heavy user, and instead of putting up boundaries, she pulled me deeper into the life I was already drowning in. What started with me offering them ounces of meth to sell quickly spiraled into something far more destructive. Soon, I was doing drugs *with* them, and then came perhaps the darkest moment of all.

One day, I found myself sitting in my bedroom, smoking crack with my mother.

Just writing that sentence haunts me. I don't know how it happened exactly. It wasn't premeditated. She was using, I was using, and suddenly, there we were, sharing a pipe in the same room.

We both knew it was wrong. We didn't say anything, but the silence was deafening. There was no screaming, no confrontation. Just shame—a deep, heavy, mutual shame.

That night didn't stop me. On the contrary, it gave me permission. Somehow, seeing her cross that line made me feel like I could cross it again. And I did. Over and over. I started selling meth more aggressively just to feed my crack addiction. I'd spend my nights getting high, crash for a few hours, then get up and do it all again. The days blurred together. The money came easy. The pain came easier.

Eventually, my body started to break down. I lost weight rapidly, and my teeth began to fall out. I was hallucinating regularly. What we called "shadow people" in the drug world, I know now are demons. Literal, spiritual tormentors. I would try to sleep and fall into what felt like a pit, a bottomless hell, only to jolt awake gasping, terrified.

One day, my mom stormed into my room. She slapped me hard and said, "You've got to get your life together."

It was a wake-up call, one of the only ones I got from her during that season, and somehow, it pierced the fog. I stopped smoking crack, but instead, I went deeper into meth. I know how crazy that sounds, replacing one drug with another, but in my twisted logic, meth was the lesser evil. Crack was killing me fast, but meth just kept me numb.

Somewhere in the haze, I started trying to claw my way back again. By this time, Robert and I had become tight. I bounced between trying to live clean and falling right back into the pit. Kelly, my high school sweetheart, was still in the picture too.

She'd show up and disappear like a ghost—one minute helping me stay grounded, the next breaking my heart.

There were glimmers of hope, but they never lasted long. I would start going back to church, then I'd relapse. I'd get sober for a few weeks, then crash harder than before. It was a cycle of chaos and craving, of wanting out and diving back in.

By the time I was nineteen, my mom had seen enough, and she kicked me out, too. Both of my parents in turn had now kicked me out of their respective homes. Once again, I had nowhere to go.

THE DOUBLE LIFE

When my mom kicked me out, I didn't have many options left. Fortunately, my brother was still living for God, still married with kids, and he opened his door to me. I slept on his couch for a few months, trying to convince myself that I could turn my life around.

It felt like maybe I could. I started going to church with him again. I got a job. I cleaned up—on the outside, at least. I even smiled more, like I believed in the version of myself I was pretending to be. But I was still using. I didn't use publicly. There was no more partying until dawn or wild nights with the crew. I wasn't smoking meth with strangers anymore, but I was smoking it alone, in secret, and lying to everyone I loved, especially Kelly.

Our relationship had come full circle. After everything I'd put her through, somehow, I was back in her family's good graces. I asked her father for permission to marry her, and he said yes. She said yes too.

To them, I looked like I'd changed. To be fair, I did a good job of playing the part, but beneath the surface, the addiction never left. I just learned to hide it better.

Eventually, my brother's small apartment got too cramped, and it was time for me to move on. He had his family to care for, and I was still camped out on his couch with no end in sight.

That's when Kelly's parents stepped in again and offered me a place to stay in their motor home parked out back.

It was a strange arrangement. I was grateful, but the environment was tense. Living that close, yet still on the outside, only added pressure to a relationship already straining under the weight of my secrets. So, Kelly and I decided to get our own place together.

With the help of her parents, we secured a loan and moved into a trailer just up the road. It was a fresh start in a new space, and a chance to finally do things right—or so I told myself. Her dad even offered me a job as a project manager for his company. It came with a company vehicle, a steady income, and a sense of status I hadn't had in years.

From the outside, things looked great. We were planning a wedding. We were building a life. But I was still using. I was staying up all night, using meth like it was oxygen, and with that came the inevitable return to my old habits.

I got back in touch with Rob Dogg. By now, he and the boys were deep into the drug game. I slipped back into that world like I'd never left. Only now, I was smarter. I began dealing wholesale. I set up my own distribution network and found people who would move product for me. I played the part of a manager by day and a drug kingpin by night.

The money rolled in fast, stacked high, but so did the lies. The cracks in my new life started to show. Kelly began to see the signs. I was disappearing for long stretches, not answering my phone. I would come home late, or not at all. When I did show up, I had cash I couldn't explain and energy I couldn't hide. She wasn't naive. She had lived through this version of me before.

Looking back now, I realize I wasn't just repeating my own mistakes—I was repeating my father's. The same rise and fall, the same fast money and faster destruction. It's like that cycle had been written into me, and I was just reading the script.

Kelly and I started fighting constantly. We fought about small things, big things, and everything in between. The wedding date felt like a countdown to confrontation. Still, we moved forward. We had set the date: July 10, 2004.

Invitations were sent, and plans were made. We got the dress, the venue, and the vows. Everything was lined up. On paper, it looked like I had rebuilt my life, but my life was a house of cards built on a foundation of lies, and soon it would all come crashing down in a way that would destroy my life.

THE FIREWORKS THAT NEVER FADED

Everything was in place. Kelly and I had the guest list, and the wedding invitations were sent out. The venue was booked, the caterers confirmed, and the pastor was lined up. A few hundred people were planning to attend. July 10 was going to be the day we turned the page. The day all of this pain would become part of the testimony we'd tell one day.

Around that time, I invited Robert into our home. Robert was getting into trouble out in Wichita, messing around with drugs, drifting like I had. I thought maybe I could help him. I knew what it was like to be lost, and I figured a fresh start might help him find his footing, so I brought him into our world.

For a while, it was good. We were like brothers, hanging out, staying up late, getting high together. We shared a lot. We talked about our pain, our regrets, our memories. We even cried together once or twice. He was solid in the way only another broken person can be. I loved him like family. We grew close enough that I asked him to be my best man.

As the wedding day approached, we decided to take a trip up to Rampart Range in Colorado. Just the two of us, dirt bikes, and drugs. It was a mountain bachelor party. We loaded up on mushrooms and rode through the forest trails for hours. Down miles and miles of winding dirt, trees whispering in the breeze, we were just two guys trying to escape the weight of real life.

We had already been up for at least a day, maybe more. The timeline is blurry. Eventually, I told him we needed to head back. "My mom's throwing a Fourth of July party tonight," I said. "Let's get cleaned up and go."

We rolled back into town hours later than we planned, somewhere around five in the afternoon. I dropped Robert off at my mom's house, then headed home to shower. When I got there, I realized Kelly was already at the party, so I cleaned up, put on a good face, and went to join the celebration.

My mom's Fourth of July parties were legendary: loud, wild, and packed with family and friends. There was plenty of fireworks, music, and backyard chaos. I always loved them, though the last two years I'd somehow managed to get arrested before the night was over. This year, I told myself, would be different. This year, I would behave. I'd respect my mom and keep it together.

However, from the moment I arrived, something felt off. It was the way Kelly and Robert looked at each other. They were strangely casual and close. I'd catch them alone in a room, or laughing a little too long, or sitting too close on the couch. Their legs would touch, and they wouldn't move. Though I wasn't a jealous person, my intuition started setting off alarm bells.

As the night wore on, my suspicion grew. Finally, the three of us were all out in the garage, the sun long gone, the sky already lit with the distant echo of fireworks. I was drunk, exhausted, and riding the edge of a two-day bender, but I wasn't numb. So I confronted them.

"What's going on?" I asked. "Why are you two always alone? Why are you acting like this?"

They looked at each other. Then they looked at me.

And they confessed. They had been sleeping together.

The words hit like a sucker punch to the soul. I couldn't tell which betrayal hurt more—hers or his. My fiancée. My best man. The woman I was about to marry. The brother I had taken in, trusted, covered for, and loved.

Something inside me snapped. I felt the switch flip. A cold, familiar fury arose, but it was sharpened by heartbreak. For a moment, I was back in all my worst places at once—strung out, abandoned, humiliated, ready to destroy anything in reach.

Then I remembered where I was. My mom's house. I'd promised myself I wouldn't ruin another holiday for her, so I turned around and walked out.

Kelly and Robert tried to stop me. They called after me, trying to talk me down, but I was done. I didn't say much. Just muttered, "Screw you. I'm done." I climbed into my truck, slammed the door, and peeled out.

I had no plan, and nowhere to put all the pain that was crashing in around me.

COLLISION COURSE

The neighborhood curled into a quiet cul-de-sac, but I came tearing out like a storm, rage boiling in my chest. Everything inside me was burning. Years of pent-up anger and trauma came out at this very moment, boiling over like a pot set on high heat too long. I didn't care who got hurt. In fact, some twisted part of me *wanted* someone to get hurt. I wanted blood. I wanted destruction.

Robert—my boy, my brother in every way but blood—had betrayed me. We'd suffered together, wept together, survived some of the ugliest years of our lives side by side. I'd brought him into my home to help him start over. Instead, he slept with my fiancée. And Kelly—the woman I had asked to marry me, despite the warning I'd heard from God years earlier—had stabbed me in the back.

I didn't see it clearly then, but I see it now. God had warned me. I hadn't listened.

Now I was speeding into the night, fully possessed by that old, familiar spirit of rage. Three red lights flew past. I didn't even slow down. My hands gripped the wheel; my foot pressed the gas like it was trying to punish the earth.

It was close to 1:00 a.m., and I was flying through Westminster, Colorado. I crested the top of 92nd Avenue where it meets Sheridan Boulevard. From the hilltop, I looked ahead and saw nothing but darkness, silence, and a red light glowing in defiance. I didn't care. I dropped my foot harder.

I must've hit ninety-five miles an hour. And then—just as the nose of my truck blew through the intersection—he appeared.

A small, older model Chevy Blazer was headed through the intersection. I remember every detail: black and gray, the driver alone, window down, wind in his hair. He was older—maybe in his fifties—and smiling. *Smiling*. Like life was still kind to him.

I hit him. Driver's side. Full speed.

As metal crumpled and glass exploded, I felt something wrap around me. It felt like a *presence*. A cocoon of peace, of stillness, of divine restraint. It was like being held. I should've died—I know that—but I didn't.

The truck spun violently. I hit the curb hard enough to shear off the back tire. A gas can from the bed flew nearly a hundred yards down the road. Debris scattered in every direction, and then—silence.

I opened the door and stumbled out. The moment my feet hit the ground, I collapsed on the curb and passed out.

Sirens woke me. Then nothing. Then again white lights. Medics leaning over me. Voices. Hands. Something cold. Then nothing.

The next time I opened my eyes, I was in an ambulance. Then the hospital. Then handcuffed to the bed. Two officers stood nearby. They didn't look angry, just stunned. They started asking me questions about the wreck, about what was in my truck, and that's when it hit me—what I had been carrying.

We'd taken a full load of weapons up to Rampart Range for target shooting. I never unpacked them. Some were legal. Some weren't. There were twelve-gauge shells strewn across the highway like confetti. A bottle of liquor had exploded in the console, soaking everything with the stench of alcohol. And then there was the meth. I had a *half pound* of meth hidden in the speaker box, along with a scale, dozens of baggies, pills, weed, a pipe, and cash—thousands in dirty money. All of it was in that truck.

To the cops, I wasn't just some reckless kid who ran a red light. I was a walking crime scene. Oddly, I had no criminal history—nothing on paper except a stint in a youth psychiatric unit. They must've wondered, *Who is this guy?*

Every time I regained consciousness, I asked the same thing: "Is the other driver okay?"

They kept telling me yes. "He's fine," they said. "He's okay."

And I believed them. Maybe I just needed to.

Once I had recovered enough physically, they transferred me from the hospital to detox. There, between cold sweats and withdrawal, I met with investigators.

They pressed hard.

"Whose drugs are these?"

"Who do the guns belong to?"

I said nothing except, "I want a lawyer."

That shut things down for the moment. The next day, they took me to county jail.

I remember walking through those doors, still in a fog. The weight of what had happened hadn't fully landed yet. The wedding, obviously, was off. My girl was gone. My future had been shattered. I'd gone from planning a life to facing years behind bars, and it still didn't feel real.

A few days later, Kelly came to visit me. We sat on opposite sides of the glass, phone in hand, trying to put words to something that had no explanation. We were two broken people, staring at the wreckage we'd both helped create. But the truth was clearer than ever. I wasn't in control. I never had been. I was a man on a collision course with God.

WARNINGS I DIDN'T LISTEN TO

Four years before that crash, I'd heard the voice of God. He was clear and unmistakable. He told me not to keep pursuing Kelly. It's not because she was evil or because I was doomed, but because God saw something I didn't. He saw what was coming, and He tried to protect me.

I didn't listen. I thought if I worked hard enough, played the part long enough, cleaned up just enough around the edges, it would all work out. I didn't need God's help. I had my own plan. My own pride.

And now I found myself in a prison cell, staring at the ruin of my life, Kelly's life, my parents' lives, and of course, the life of the man I hit with my truck. His name was Steven. He deserves to be remembered, not as a footnote in my story, but as a man whose life intersected mine in one of the most tragic, consequential moments.

The truth about double lives is that they always end in collapse. When you live one version of yourself in public and another in secret, the person you're really fooling is yourself. Everyone else sees through the cracks eventually. God never bought the act.

Sadly, addiction is a beast that builds a home inside your bones. It becomes your rhythm and your need. I remember a night when Kelly and I were living in the trailer together—long before the crash, long before jail. I was deep into meth, and I suddenly realized my supply had dried up.

I couldn't get my next hit. My contacts had nothing, and I became desperate. In that drought, I learned just how strong the hook of meth had become. For the first time, I admitted to myself, "I can't stop this." I wasn't in control. Meth was. I would've done anything to get more. That was the moment I realized I might be an addict forever, and that thought scared me like nothing else had.

Addiction takes and takes, and it doesn't ask permission. The first thing it steals is your ability to imagine life without it. That moment in the trailer with the empty stash was a warning, but like all the others, I ignored it. I thought I was strong. I thought I was smarter than the drug. But addiction isn't about weakness or intelligence. It's about spiritual bondage.

CHAPTER SEVEN

THE BELLY OF THE BEAST

WAKING UP IN JAIL IS A STRANGE THING. THERE'S NO ALARM clock, no light switch, no sense of the hour—just the chill of a concrete floor and the cold weight of your reality hitting you. When I opened my eyes that first morning behind bars, the craziness of what had just happened hadn't fully caught up with me. But the haze of drugs and drunken rage was lifting, and I remember thinking, with vivid clarity, *I really messed up.*

The wedding was off. That was obvious. Kelly wasn't wearing the ring anymore, and neither of us had the strength to pretend that "someday" was still coming. Life as I knew it had utterly fallen apart, and not gently, but like a building gutted by fire.

Over the next few days in jail, the wretchedness of it all began to settle like dust. Kelly came to visit. Her parents came. So did mine. Every face wore the same expression of hurt, anger, and disappointment, and I understood why. I didn't have any defense left. All I could do was sit there behind the glass, trying not to completely lose it while they looked at me like a stranger.

I felt numb, but not in the way drugs numb you. This was a spiritual numbness—a kind of lostness that went deeper than pain. It was like I had fallen into a pit so dark that I couldn't even remember what the sun looked like. I'd been running from God for four and a half years, sliding further and further down into the darkness, even as I tried to pretend I had it all under control.

And now, at last, I was done pretending. I was done lying to myself.

About five days into my time there, I heard that there was going to be a chapel service. A volunteer pastor was coming in to speak to any inmates who wanted to attend. There were maybe four or five of us in the room. It wasn't much of a church service by outward standards. There was no stained glass, no steeple, no booming choir—just a folding table, a cracked-open Bible, and a small CD player playing worship music quietly in the background. But something holy happened there. As I sat in that plastic chair under those flickering fluorescent lights, the room seemed to fade away. I wasn't in jail anymore. I wasn't facing decades of consequences or surrounded by my failures. I was alone with God.

And then I heard it. That voice. The same still, small voice I had heard nearly five years earlier. The one I had ignored when it told me not to pursue a relationship that would later come to define some of my deepest pain.

This time, the voice didn't warn me. It simply asked, "Rick, are you done?"

That was it. No fire. No thunder. Just a quiet question that cut deeper than any punishment ever could, and I broke. Tears ran down my face. My chest heaved. My soul gave out. And I whispered, "Yes, I'm done."

I meant it. In that moment, I surrendered everything: my plans, my pain, my pride. I gave my heart back to God, and somehow, even in that dark, dingy room surrounded by inmates and guarded by men with badges, I felt free.

Maybe you're someone who's been running from God, trying to do life on your own. If that's you, I want to offer a prayer and a glimpse of hope. God is not mad at you. He's not waiting for you to return so He can punish you. He's waiting with open arms, ready to love you and welcome you back. It took me a lifetime of pain to realize that. Maybe this moment is *your* chance to realize it too.

Three days later, something unexpected happened. It was midnight. A guard walked over and called my name. "Scadden. Pack your stuff. You're getting out."

I sat up, dazed. "What?"

"You're out. Let's go."

There was no explanation and no paperwork. I had no bond money. Except for some pocket change, all of my cash had been confiscated in the wreck, along with the drugs, guns, and everything else I didn't want to remember. My mom didn't have the money, and Kelly definitely wasn't going to post bail. As far as I knew, nobody was coming for me, but somehow, I was walking free.

They didn't let me call anyone or offer me a ride. They just opened the jail door and released me into the night. I didn't know where to go. I didn't know what I would say to anyone, so I just started walking through the silence of early morning. The same thought kept running through my head: *I should be dead, but I'm not. I'm still here.*

Back then, there were still pay phones on the street. I walked for miles until I found one. Then I used the change in my pocket to make a call.

First, I called Kelly and told her I was out, but she refused to come pick me up. She told me she couldn't, though she didn't explain why. So I called my dad.

He came quickly and quietly, picked me up without asking too many questions, and drove me home to the house Kelly and I had shared. The porch light was on. I remember thinking that was strange. Inside, the washer was running, and Kelly was folding bedsheets at three in the morning. I knew something wasn't right.

She said she couldn't pick me up from jail, but now here she was—wide awake and working on laundry in the middle of the night like she was expecting someone else. At that moment, I knew—Robert had been staying there.

Even in my half-sober fog, I could feel it, that gut feeling you can't quite explain but you know it's true. Robert was staying in my house, sleeping in my bed. While my life was still in shards and ash, they had just kept going. That cut deeper than any cell door ever could.

WORSE NEWS

A few days later, an old, familiar friend showed up at my door with a grin on his face and a package in his hand. "It was me," he said. "I bonded you out."

He then handed me a pound of meth.

"Go get a lawyer," he said.

I had just recommitted my life to Christ in jail. Five days earlier, I was in a rickety prison chapel, crying out to God with everything I had left. And now, here I was, standing on my own doorstep, a fresh pound of meth in my hand. The devil is always knocking. The question is, are you going to let him in? I did. I opened the door wide and started using again. That's how powerful old sinful habits are. They don't let go so easily, no matter how much damage has been done.

Over the next few weeks, the pieces of my old life kept falling away. Kelly moved out. Her parents cut ties. One by one, everything that had looked like my future disappeared, and I found myself in the darkness once again. More meth. More booze. More nights I couldn't remember. More mornings I wished I couldn't.

I was spiraling again, but I needed money, and I needed something to do. My dad—God bless him—hired me back at his painting company. It gave me something to do, somewhere to be. It gave me a break from the haunting quiet of my house and the demons that lived there. And it provided a sliver of structure while I waited for the court system to decide what would happen to me.

My lawyer didn't sugarcoat it. "This case doesn't look good," he told me, "but if you can keep your nose clean—literally and figuratively—there's a chance you won't get much prison time."

I latched onto that hope like a man clinging to driftwood.

And then, one day, the phone rang. We were on a job in downtown Denver. I was standing in a stairwell when I saw the caller ID light up. It was my attorney. I picked up, and his voice was flat.

"Rick," he said, "I've got some bad news."

I laughed a little, hollow and dry. "Worse than what I'm already facing?"

He didn't hesitate. "The DA has dropped the charge of vehicular assault. They're filing new charges: vehicular homicide. Steven passed away. The guy you hit, he's gone. I'm sorry."

The world slowed down. My breath caught somewhere between my chest and my throat, and for a moment, everything was utterly quiet—the kind of quiet that comes from devastation.

I killed someone. I took a life. With my truck. My choices. My stubbornness and pride and rebellion.

I hung up the phone and called for my dad. When he came running down the stairs, I collapsed into his arms and wept. We stood there for half an hour, me holding onto him like a child, sobbing, shaking, crushed by a kind of grief I didn't know existed. This was the kind of soul-breaking sorrow that scrapes you hollow and leaves nothing behind.

Eventually the tears dried up. I pulled away, wiped my eyes, and told him I was leaving. And that was the beginning of the next spiral.

The logic in my mind was simple, even if it was twisted: *If I'm going to prison forever, I might as well live like hell until I get there.* I wish I could say I resisted. I didn't. I leaned in hard.

The irony wasn't lost on me. My dad had once wrecked his own life in a car, high and drunk and wild. I had seen that pattern play out, and I had vowed not to repeat it. Yet here I was, trapped in the same story, replaying it beat for beat.

RUNNING FROM THE WRECKAGE INSIDE

My dad had run from his crimes. He skipped court dates, dodged responsibility, ducked behind addiction like it could shield him from consequence. I didn't do that. I was spiraling, but I kept my court dates and checked the boxes the system gave me. That didn't mean I was clean.

An "F it" attitude had me tight in its grip. Somewhere deep down, I figured the damage was already done so I might as well burn the rest down while I still had matches to spare. I was drinking every night, smoking meth every day, but it didn't stop there. I began robbing homes, meeting up with hookers, picking up strangers, running from one high to the next, as if speed and sex could smother the wreckage inside me. I was reckless in every sense of the word. I didn't care if the sun rose or if I made it home.

Of course, the law caught up to me. Twice, I was arrested for second-degree, nonresidential burglary. Both times, somehow—God only knows how—I was released on personal recognizance bonds the next day. It was like the system hadn't realized yet how badly I was crashing, or maybe they hadn't connected all the cases. Maybe God was giving me another chance, or maybe the enemy was just buying me more rope to hang myself.

Then came the night in the hotel room.

I was with a woman I barely knew. We were high, naked, tangled in the sheets. Suddenly, there came a heavy pounding on the door. I peeked through the window and saw six cops standing outside, hands on holsters, yelling for us to open up.

I panicked and ran around the room, stuffing drugs under pillows, shoving paraphernalia into drawers, but it was no use. They busted in and cuffed us both. Then they went down to my truck and searched it, where they found another illegal gun—a .40 caliber Desert Eagle. They also found baggies, scales, everything.

I was taken to Denver County Jail. While in the holding cell, they gave me one phone call. I dialed my mom and told her exactly where the truck was and that I needed her to retrieve it—specifically, the money hidden inside.

"Use it to bond me out," I said. "But do it quick—before they figure out who I really am and what I'm already out on bond for."

Somehow, she pulled it off. By the time the authorities realized I was already facing charges in Thornton and elsewhere, I was already out again.

My lawyer was furious. "They're going to revoke your bond," he said. "You understand that, right?"

I nodded, numb.

At the next hearing, the judge issued a warning. "One more mistake," she said, "and you're not walking out of this courtroom again."

I believed her. I did. But belief didn't keep me clean.

At some point in all this, I started dating Robert's ex-girlfriend, Jenny. Maybe I was being petty, trying to get revenge. Or it might have just been another bad decision on a growing list. One day she asked if I wanted to go with her to Kansas for her grandfather's birthday. I knew it was illegal to leave the state while out on bond, but I rationalized it. My court date was a week away, and I wasn't scheduled for any drug tests. I told myself I'd be fine.

We hit the road. Of course, we were high, and neither of us had slept in twenty-four hours. We made it as far as Salina, Kansas, when the lights lit up behind us.

It was strange from the start. Jenny was driving, but the trooper came to *my* window. "License and ID," he said flatly.

Even high, I knew what was happening. I stepped out, and before I could process it, the cuffs were back on.

Someone had tipped them off. Maybe the bondsman. I was under a $50,000 bond back in Colorado, and no bondsman is going to risk that kind of money on a guy who can't even stay sober across state lines.

I was taken to the local jail in Salina. According to extradition laws, Colorado had ten days to come get me. If they didn't, I'd be released. So I watched the clock every day,

While I was there, I called my dad, and my father, of all people, spoke a blessing over my life. "Someday," he said, "God will restore everything to you just like Job in the Scriptures." I couldn't see it at the time, but years later, when my son was born, I knew—that was it. That was the blessing my dad spoke over me coming to life.

At that time, however, I was mostly worrying about extradition. However, days went by, and no one showed up to get me. By day nine, I was confident. "They're not coming," I said. "They forgot about me."

And then, at 11:50 p.m.—ten minutes before the deadline—a bus pulled into the lot. They hadn't forgotten. I was loaded up for extradition—shackled, processed, and placed on what I thought would be a short ride back to Colorado.

I thought wrong.

SENTENCED, BUT SET FREE

I assumed I'd ride back to Colorado, face the music, and begin the long road toward whatever redemption might look like, but the ride wasn't quick. It wasn't even direct. Instead of heading west, the prison bus went east, and for three weeks, I lived in chains.

We crisscrossed the country, stopping at jails to pick up other inmates, eating cold meals at roadside holding facilities, riding through night and day in a steel cage. I slept upright on plastic seats. I saw sunrises through barred windows, and with every mile, the shame set in deeper. Don't feel sorry for me—I earned every bit of that misery—but it broke me in ways I couldn't fully comprehend at the time.

By the time I returned to Adams County, the system had already moved on. I'd missed my court dates so warrants had been issued. Even though my mom tried calling the courts to explain, it was too late. In the pod that day, when I heard I'd missed the deadline and that my bond was gone for good, I finally gave up.

That's when I said, "God, I'm done. I'm yours," and I finally, fully meant it.

Yes, I'd said those words before. I'd made promises and broken them, but this time felt different. I didn't pray to get out. I wasn't asking for a miracle. I just wanted to be made new, even if that meant being made new in a prison cell. I started reading my Bible again and praying. I found other inmates to pray with. I wasn't trying to impress anyone. After all, there wasn't anyone to impress. I just knew I didn't want to keep living as two different people.

The court dates resumed. I showed up and sat in shackles, answering all of their questions. And then came the day that would define the rest of my life—my sentencing.

Six months had passed since extradition. Once again, my lawyer didn't sugarcoat it. "Rick," he said, "with the new charges you picked up, we could be looking at anywhere from twelve to twenty-four years, maybe more. If the judge runs the sentences consecutively, you could be staring down thirty-plus."

I barely slept the night before. That morning, they walked me into a small holding cell with another inmate. We were both on the docket. He paced, but I sat still, silent, praying.

They called my name.

Walking into a courtroom to hear your sentence is like stepping in front of a firing squad that hasn't made up its mind yet. The judge becomes more than a person—he becomes time itself, holding your future in the folds of a manila folder. My stomach turned as I sat down.

We'd taken a plea. There wasn't much to contest. I was guilty. According to the deal, I would plead to vehicular homicide, burglary, and drug possession. In exchange, the prosecution would drop a special offender charge—a federal enhancement for having drugs and guns together, which would've guaranteed me a federal sentence and possibly decades behind bars.

Twelve to twenty-four years was the range. If they ran my sentences *concurrent*—that is, at the same time—I would serve twelve. If they ran them *consecutively*, I was looking at thirty-three years.

The judge read the charges one by one.

"Vehicular homicide," he said, "twelve years in the Department of Corrections."

My throat tightened.

"Second-degree burglary: eight years. Schedule-two drug possession with intent to distribute: eight years. Schedule-two drug possession with intent to distribute: five years. All to be served concurrently, with a mandatory five years parole."

So, all told, I would serve twelve years total, plus five years of mandatory parole once I got out.

My response at that moment surprised me. Instead of feeling horrified, I felt relief. The second the judge handed down the sentence, it was like a weight slid off my back. Not because twelve years is easy or because I thought prison would be some retreat. No, but for the first time in a long time, there was a clear line in the sand. The chaos of waiting, of hiding, of spiraling was over. I wasn't guessing anymore. I knew what I was facing, so I could finally breathe. It's strange to say it, but being sentenced didn't feel like the end of my life. It felt like the start of one.

I remember thinking, *Maybe now I can finally begin to heal.* Maybe now, I could step into the painful but necessary journey of rehabilitation, of owning up to what I had done, and serving the time I deserved. I had taken a life—an innocent man's life—and there was no excuse or justification that could change that. I knew in my heart that prison time was a debt I had to pay. Honestly, to me, twelve years didn't seem long enough to make up for the loss of an innocent life.

It wasn't until later, deep into the legal process, that I learned who Steven really was. He wasn't just a stranger. He was the son of a retired district judge from Adams County—a well-known man with deep ties to the very system that would now decide my fate. When that truth came to light, I braced myself for the worst. I thought, *There's no way they're going to show me mercy. Not after this.*

But somehow, they did. I don't say that lightly. I don't chalk that up to good luck or legal maneuvering. That was God's hand on my life. There's no other explanation. I was spared from what could have been a much harsher sentence.

I felt grateful—though it feels strange to say it—that Steven didn't leave behind a wife or children. His death was still a tragedy. I will carry that truth with me for the rest of my life, but it gave me the smallest sliver of relief to know that I hadn't torn a father away from his kids or a husband from his wife.

After I was sentenced, I returned to the holding cell filled with hope. Not despair or fear but real, honest hope. The other inmate looked at me and asked, "How much time did you get?"

"Twelve years," I replied.

He sank back like the wind had been knocked out of him, like I had just told him he was about to face death itself. Most guys break down when they get hit with a sentence like that. Some lash out. Others shut down. Some even try to take their own lives. Jail staff are trained to keep a close eye on men like that.

But I felt peace. It wasn't a peace that made sense. No, this was the kind the Bible talks about—the peace that surpasses all understanding. I couldn't explain it, but I knew it wasn't from me. It was from Jesus. That day marked a turning point for me.

My old life was over, but a new life shaped by faith, responsibility, and redemption was just beginning.

THROUGH THE GATES

After my sentencing, I was sent back to county jail to await my transport to prison. A few months later, in June 2005, they called my name. It was time. I packed up my things and boarded the transport to prison.

I had no idea where I was going. For security reasons, they don't tell you. It's a terrifying experience. You're stepping into the unknown with nothing but a prison number and a prayer. I ended up at the Denver Reception and Diagnostic Center (DRDC), which is a processing hub where inmates from all across Colorado are sent for intake. While there, they assess you, assign your custody level, and then decide where to send you permanently.

Walking through those gates, I felt like I was stepping into a movie. They stripped me of everything: my clothes, my hair, my identity. They sprayed me down with something (iodine, I think) and handed me my new uniform. Just like that, I was no longer who I'd been. I was an inmate with a number instead of a name.

From there, the system ran on points. Based on the crimes you committed, they calculate your total score, and that number determines the level of security you're assigned. While I was waiting to be assigned, the other inmates in DRDC swapped horror stories about the awful places you could be sent: Sterling, Buena Vista, Limon. One of the worst, they said, was Burlington. Technically, the Kit Carson Correctional Facility, it had a bad reputation as a poorly run, privately owned dump.

Anywhere but there, I prayed.

And of course, I got Burlington.

It was tucked away in the farthest reaches of eastern Colorado. The ride out there wasn't even on a full bus—just a van. Those hours were quiet, and I felt completely isolated, even though there were eight of us crammed together in that vehicle. It was like God was giving me space to think, pray, and brace for whatever lay ahead. Some of the guys had been to prison before. Others, like me, were walking into the unknown.

When we got to Burlington, they rushed us to our pod. The second the door opened, the sounds hit me like a wall. Inmates yelling, metal clanging, someone in the back laughing and shouting, *"Fresh meat!"* They were joking, but it didn't feel like a joke at the time, not to someone who'd never been there before.

My room was up the stairs. I met my new cellmate. He seemed decent enough, but prison comes with its own set of rules. There are the rules the guards enforce, and then there are the unspoken ones that inmates live by. One of those is the *paperwork check*. It's a way inmates police each other and weed out the ones they consider unforgivable (child molesters, rapists, etc.).

So, I handed over my paperwork and told the other inmates what I was in for. I passed. I was "clean" in their eyes. That doesn't mean you're safe, but it means you've got one less target on your back.

At the time, I had a shaved head. It was just easier that way. I didn't know anything about prison barbers or rules around haircuts. I figured, why not keep it simple? That decision nearly got me killed.

A couple days in, I stepped out of my cell with my shower gear. I hadn't even made it down the stairs before I saw one of the leaders of the Aryan Brotherhood in our pod. He was a big man, with eyes that looked through you. He didn't say a word at first. He just grabbed his shower stuff and followed me.

We stood side by side in the shower area, and I knew something was coming.

He started talking casually, asking things like, "Where you from? What are you in for?" Then he got to the real question: "Are you affiliated?"

"No, man," I said. "I'm just doing my own thing."

He nodded, then looked me dead in the eyes.

"Then you can't have a shaved head. That's for us. You need to grow your hair back."

He didn't have to say more than that. I knew what he meant. It wasn't a suggestion. In prison, affiliation is survival. Wearing the wrong look, saying the wrong thing, or sitting in the wrong seat can cost you your life, and in that moment, over something as simple as a haircut, I thought I might get shanked.

So I nodded and said, "Yes, sir. Say no more. Hair growth starts today."

That was prison. Rules on top of rules, both spoken and unspoken. The violence wasn't constant, but it always simmered beneath the surface. Fights broke out often enough, and tension never left the pod. You lived every day on alert, with your eyes open, your heart guarded, and your back to the wall when possible. You are never fully relaxed.

Prison teaches you the art of silence. You learn fast how to mind your business and keep your head down. I learned that lesson the hard way, at a pinochle table of all places.

In prison, card games are more than just pastimes. They're rituals. You've got spades, poker, and, in our pod, pinochle. That's what filled the empty hours and kept us from going crazy. Me and my partner were pretty good, and we were winning game after game against some tough competition. On this particular day, we were up against two big guys—hard men who carried weight in the pod. Once again, we were winning, and that didn't sit well with one of them.

The tension started to simmer. He was cussing, slamming his cards, accusing us of cheating. His partner started making clumsy plays, and that only fueled his frustration. Then, without warning, the man stood up, walked around the table, and cold-cocked his own partner—just dropped him with a single punch right there in front of us.

It happened fast. There was no warning, no words exchanged.

Just a fist and a fall. My partner and I didn't say a word. We didn't flinch. We calmly stood up from the table and walked away like it never happened.

That's what you do in prison. You don't react. You don't ask questions. And you *definitely* don't tell the guards. There's nothing worse, or more dangerous, than being a snitch in prison. If you want to survive, you have to keep your peace and keep your distance. That mindset kept me alive through five and a half years behind bars.

But even in that pressure cooker, God began to fulfill his calling in my life. I started leading prayer circles and sharing Scripture. I still believed that God hadn't just saved me *from* something but *for* something. I was a pastor now, even if I didn't carry the title, and my congregation was made up of the forgotten, the broken, and the desperate—just like I had been.

FROM THE KILL FENCE TO BOOT CAMP

Every six months, the prison system reevaluates you. They look at your record: Have you been in fights? Are you going to classes? Are you doing the work? Based on that, your points rise or fall, and your points determine where you serve. A year into my time at Burlington, my points dropped enough to qualify me for transfer to a lower-security facility.

They sent me to Sterling Correctional Facility way up in the northeast corner of the state. Now, Sterling has a reputation. It's the largest prison in Colorado and the only one surrounded by a so-called *kill fence*. If you somehow manage to climb through twelve layers of razor wire and fencing, you'd still have to contend with that final, lethal barrier. No one escapes Sterling.

I was assigned to the minimum-restrictive side, which gave me a bit more breathing room, and I kept on doing what God had called me to do. I went to chapel, led Bible studies, and constantly encouraged the men around me.

One day I heard about a boot camp program run by the Department of Corrections in Buena Vista. If you completed the intensive three-month course, you could go before a judge and request a reconsideration of your sentence. For some, it meant early release. I figured, *What do I have to lose?* So I applied, and I got accepted.

Six months into Sterling, I packed up again, this time headed for Buena Vista. The transfer was rough—a long ride all the way across the state, probably six hours or so. We stopped at a small county jail in Park County overnight, where I was placed in a temporary holding cell for inmates en route to the next stop in their journey.

The next morning, we boarded the bus. I still remember that bus *vividly*. It looked and smelled like it hadn't been cleaned since the Reagan administration. The windows were busted out, the vinyl seats torn to the springs. It was barely roadworthy, but it only had one job: to deliver us to the gates of one of the most intense environments I would ever face.

As we rolled through the gates of the prison yard in Buena Vista, the air seemed to change. The minute those heavy steel gates slammed shut behind us, I knew something bad was coming.

Then they appeared. Fifty drill-sergeant-style officers came marching out of the building, boots hitting the pavement like drumbeats. They marched straight for our bus. I could feel the blood drain from my face. My hands went clammy. I'd been through sentencing, through intake, through prison violence, but nothing had prepared me for that moment.

They reached the bus and started screaming. Not yelling—*screaming*. Barking orders, demanding compliance, tearing down every shred of ego we had left.

It was boot camp, alright, but not the kind you see in motivational videos. This was about control and discipline. The goal was to break you down to build you into someone the system could manage. And yet, even in that chaos, I clung to one truth: God still had me, and I still had a calling.

The drill sergeants screamed like demons the moment the bus doors swung open: "Get off the bus!" "No—get back on!" "Hit the ground!" "Drop and give me fifty!"

It was chaos wrapped in discipline. Imagine five drill sergeants in your face at once, hats pressed against your forehead, spittle flying, voices like thunder cracking in your ears. One minute they had you running laps around the building, the next you were face down in the dirt, then back on your feet and moving again before you could catch your breath.

Welcome to prison boot camp.

HELL WEEK AND HOLY GROUND

I'd been locked up for over a year and a half by then, and I was in decent shape. Some of the guys on that busted, windowless prison bus weren't. They fell apart fast. Some vomited. Others cried. Some got injured, with scraped-up knees, twisted ankles, broken arms. It was the kind of brutality that broke people, and that was the point.

This was a reeducation prison modeled after Marine Corps boot camps from the 1950s. Week one was called *Hell Week* for good reason. You stood at attention for eight, ten, sometimes twelve hours a day. That meant absolutely no movement and no speaking. If you so much as scratched your nose, you did push-ups. If your eyes drifted, more push-ups. If you even breathed wrong? You guessed it: push-ups.

You could quit at any time—the program was voluntary—and guys dropped out constantly, begging to be sent back to their "normal" prison yards, where at least they could sleep without someone screaming in their ear at 3:00 a.m. I'll be honest, there were moments I thought about quitting, too. By day four or five, standing there, sweat rolling down my back, muscles aching, throat dry—I started hearing that old voice in my head: *Why are you doing this? Go back. You don't need this. You don't belong here.*

But I couldn't give in. I had come too far and had too much to lose. I wanted early release, but more than that, I wanted some form of redemption.

Phase one turned into phase two. Phase two into phase three. Each phase was a month long. By the third month, we were machines. I could do two hundred push-ups in a row. There wasn't a drill they could throw at me that I couldn't complete. My body had been broken and rebuilt, but it wasn't the workouts that changed my life. It was *the Pit*.

The Pit was exactly what it sounds like: a fifty-yard square of gravel, dirt, and misery. It was where they took you when they *really* wanted to make a point. We called it *thrashing*. You'd bear crawl, roll, sweat, and throw up until your body gave out, and when it did, when you finally vomited from sheer exhaustion, the drill sergeants would yell, "I didn't say you could throw up on my gravel! Pick it up. Put it in your pocket!"

So you did. You scooped up your own vomit and put it in your pocket, because you didn't ask questions out there. You followed orders.

However, one day, the Pit became holy ground.

Our sergeant told us to dig basketball-sized holes. We were confused, but we obeyed. Then he told us to put our heads inside the holes—literally.

"Bury your head," he said, "but leave an air pocket. I don't want to have to carry any of you out on a stretcher."

I crouched there with my face in the dirt, breathing through a hole I dug myself. I could feel the gravel press against my cheeks. The silence was eerie.

Then it hit me: *This is your life. This is what you've made of it.*

I was a man in prison, with my head buried in the ground, literally and metaphorically, and suddenly, I wasn't just following orders. I was staring in a mirror at the absolute wreckage of my life and my choices. That moment cracked something open in me. For all the push-ups and screaming and humiliation, it was that dirt-in-your-face, stillness-before-God moment that changed my soul. I realized I didn't want to die like this. I didn't want my story to end buried in gravel.

A second turning point came later, when one of the higher-ranking officers gathered us for a talk. There was no yelling this time. In fact, he just talked to us like a regular human being. I remember he looked at us and said something that stuck with me:

"Life is about being true to yourself."

Even though it was a simple saying, that statement hit my hardened heart like a divine hammer. I had been running from myself for so long—wearing masks, hiding shame, burying pain. So much of my life up to that moment had been a performance. Outwardly, I had played roles, but inwardly, I'd lost track of who I really was.

That one sentence exposed the double life I'd been living—the man people thought I was and the man I couldn't bear to face in the mirror—and somehow, it set me free from that. It gave me permission to stop pretending, to finally show up as the real me—flawed but honest.

The Bible says, "You shall know the truth, and the truth shall set you free."[2] That's exactly what happened that night. I came face to face with the raw, personal truth I had avoided: I had betrayed myself, and now—through exhaustion, dirt, discipline, and pain—I was being called back to who I was always meant to be.

That one insight made the rest of boot camp bearable, but more importantly, it made the experience meaningful. By the time I reached phase three, I was a different man. Stronger in body, yes, but I was also clear in spirit.

---

[2] John 8:32 (English Standard Version)

Finally, graduation day arrived. This was a big deal for me. For the first time in my life, I finished something.

My family came to the ceremony. As I stood there in my uniform, I saw my mom's eyes well with tears. Remember, I had dropped out of high school, I'd quit football—I had started so many things and walked away from all of them. But I had completed prison boot camp. It was one of the proudest moments of my life.

Now, to be clear, not everything about boot camp was redemptive. Some of it was just plain cruel. Like during phase one, when they marched us into the chow hall and made us eat standing up with our eyes locked straight ahead. You couldn't look down at your food, so you had to figure out how to scoop it into your mouth without ever seeing it. And before every meal, they'd force you to drink an entire canteen of water. Guys would gag and throw up, yet they were still expected to finish their trays. It was military madness with a cruel psychological twist.

Still, I made it, and I left in the best physical shape of my life, even if I was still behind bars.

STRIVING TOWARD FREEDOM

After graduation, they shipped me off to my next prison—my fourth in just two years. This time, I landed at the Skyline Correctional Facility in East Canon Correctional Complex. If you've never heard of it, Cañon City, Colorado, is practically a prison town. Within a few square miles, there are at least seven state correctional facilities and another one in the town itself.

The prison they sent me to this time was different from the ones that came before. There were no fences or towers or razor wire—no kill fence—and you were given a key to your own cell. I couldn't believe it. The food was good. The tension was low. You didn't have to racially segregate like you did in other places. It was almost peaceful. Almost.

It was there that my ministry truly began. Because of my good behavior, I earned a rare privilege: I was allowed to serve as the chaplain's assistant. In the prison church, that's the most respected role a Christian inmate can have, not just because of status but because of access. They trusted me enough to go into the chapel alone, so I cleaned and maintained it, and I worshiped there.

Imagine being locked in prison but worshiping freely. I spent those times alone and in peace. I would turn on praise music, let it fill the space, and just spend time with God. For those few hours, I wasn't a prisoner. I was a pastor in training.

My mom came to visit regularly during that season. I was working, exercising, staying sharp, but above all, I was preparing for the hearing that had been promised back in boot camp. I would get a chance to stand before a judge once again and ask for a second chance. With my heart finally aligned with the truth, I was ready.

Finally, the day of my hearing arrived. Walking into that same courtroom felt like stepping into an entirely different world than the one I'd faced years earlier. The last time I'd stood before that judge, I was broken, skinny, hollow-eyed, and hopeless. But now, I walked in with life in my eyes. I felt stronger, healthier, and more hopeful than I'd ever been. My lawyer smiled as I approached. The courtroom felt lighter, more expectant. Everyone could see the change because it wasn't just external. Something deep inside me had transformed, and I carried *purpose* now.

The hearing moved quickly. The judge acknowledged the boot camp program I'd completed and, almost like it was nothing, knocked four years off my sentence. Just like that, twelve years became eight, which meant I was now eligible for parole and the halfway house. I could taste freedom. I walked out of that courtroom thinking, *This is it. I'm going home.*

But prison has a way of keeping you humble. When I went

before the parole board, they denied me. I applied for the halfway house and got denied again. In prison, every "no" comes with a waiting period. I had to wait six months before I could reapply for the halfway house, a full year before another parole hearing.

It was a gut punch. After all that progress, all that growth, the door didn't open, but God wasn't done.

Around that time, my caseworker approached me with a proposal. "There's a new reentry prison opening up in Colorado Springs," he said. "It's designed to help guys transition back into society."

I wasn't interested. I had heard rumors about the place, and it sounded crazy, experimental, not the kind of place I wanted to spend the next stretch of my sentence. I declined.

But prison doesn't work on consent. You don't get a vote. A week later, they transferred me there anyway.

That's something people on the outside don't always understand. In prison, you don't own anything—not your space, not your time, not even your path. You belong to the state. They can move you wherever they want, whenever they want, and you have zero say. Prison isn't just confinement—it's disempowerment. It's being cut off not just from the world, but from any illusion of control.

So, I found myself in a brand-new, privately run prison—a towering, modern structure that looked promising on the outside but was sheer human misery inside. Imagine twelve inmates packed into a single bunk room. There were fights every night, guys brewing hooch in the corners, drugs everywhere. The whole place was loud, violent, and unstable.

At first, I was disoriented—and disappointed. *Why am I here, God?* I asked more than once. However, after a couple of weeks, I realized exactly why I'd been sent there. As it turned out, there was a church inside the prison, and it was run by inmates. The man who had been leading it was on his way out, so they needed someone new to step up and carry the torch.

Just like that, God called my name. I said yes.

That tiny prison church became my training ground. I became the inmate representative—the pastor, in a way. I organized services, worked with outside ministers, and built a choir. We even started a worship band. I mentored guys, taught the Word, led prayer, and preached my heart out.

It was my first taste of what I now know was church planting. From fifteen inmates attending our little service, we grew to over a hundred, not because of me but because of what God was doing in that place. People were getting saved, healed, and delivered, and it wasn't just the inmates. One day, I looked up and saw a correctional officer sitting quietly in the back of the church service. The next week, there were more guards. They came just to sit in the presence of God.

Something holy was happening in the middle of the madness. That room inside a prison meant to warehouse the forgotten became a sanctuary. Church was loud, unpolished, and full of men with rap sheets a mile long, but it was also sacred and Spirit-filled.

I had found my purpose, and I had found it in the last place I ever expected.

Eventually, the time came for me to apply for parole and the halfway house again. I was hopeful. I thought, *Surely now's the time. I've done the work. I've served. I've led. I've honored God in this place. Surely He's going to open the door.*

But He didn't. I got denied for both again. I'll be honest with you, I didn't take it well. At first, I masked it in spiritual language. I said things like, "God must be doing something bigger. There's a reason. He's in control," but underneath, I was bitter. Deep down, I believed I had earned my way out. I thought, *God, I've been faithful. I've preached. I've built a church. I've poured myself out for You. Now it's Your turn to move.*

That's not how the kingdom works. I see it clearly now. God was exposing something in me I didn't even know was still there, a subtle pride, a belief that obedience should produce reward on my timeline. I was convinced that my service had earned me a blessing, but God doesn't work on a barter system. We don't serve Him to get something out of Him. We serve Him because we love Him.

Still, that denial wounded me. It left me jaded and distant. My faith was still there, but it was bruised.

A RIDICULOUS ACCUSATION

After a year at the reentry prison in Colorado Springs, I had the opportunity to transfer. Some guys were going home. Others, like me, were just moving on. I handed the church over to another inmate and packed up. My next stop was Delta, Colorado.

Most prisoners don't bounce around like I did, but looking back, I can see how each prison was a chapter in my calling. God used me in every one of those places, and now, even in my bitterness, He was preparing me for something more.

Delta Correctional Center was a step up. It had minimum security and bigger rooms. You got your own key, the food was good, and there were fewer restrictions. On the outside, things looked easier, but on the inside, I was hurting. I was angry at God and frustrated with the system. Mostly, I was disappointed that freedom felt so far away.

Still, I tried to rebuild my life. I made new friends and settled into a routine. In prison, routine is everything. Without it, time crawls, but with it, the days move faster. If you find rhythm, you find sanity.

A few months in, I started to feel normal again. I was making friends, working out regularly, and settling in. And then it all fell apart yet again, this time over something that had nothing to do with me or my choices.

My mom came to visit me one Saturday morning. I hadn't seen her in a while, and her visits were like oxygen—brief moments of grace from the outside world. So I was already dressed up nicely and waiting for her in my cell. I remember looking out the window and watching her walk into the building.

A minute later, I saw her walk back out of the building and leave. It was strange. Had they turned her away for some reason?

Maybe she just forgot something, I told myself.

Then there came a knock at my cell door, and a moment later, three stone-faced prison guards entered.

"Cuff up," one of them said.

I was shocked. "What? Why? What's going on?"

They didn't bother to answer. Instead, they promptly turned me around and slapped handcuffs on me. And then, with no explanation, they marched me out of my cell and took me to solitary confinement. Inmates call it "the hole." It's where they send you when they think you've done something bad, or sometimes, when they just need to figure out what to do with you. I had no idea why I was there. What could I have possibly done to deserve this?

I sat in the darkness for hours before I learned the reason. The guards thought my mom had tried to bring me drugs during visitation. It was an absurd accusation. It couldn't have been further from the truth. If it *had* been true, I promise you, I would tell you right now, in this book, but it wasn't.

Later, I found out what *really* happened. One of the prison guards had gotten too handsy during the pat-down and crossed a line. My mom flinched and told him to stop. That was enough, in their eyes, to raise suspicion. That tiny act of resistance triggered everything.

Unfortunately, it also showed me, yet again, that in prison, they can do whatever they want with you. You don't own your time. You don't have a voice. You don't get to defend yourself. You are state property, and the rules—whether spoken or unspoken—can change without notice.

Once again, I found myself at rock bottom, but once again, God was with me.

When you get sent to the hole in prison, they hold what's basically a mini trial. You go before a "judge," but it's a correction officer instead of someone in robes with a gavel. That officer has the authority to decide your fate within those walls. You get a "lawyer," too, who is usually an inmate rep who acts on your behalf, but everyone knows it's all mostly for show.

So there I was, standing before this so-called judge, trying to explain myself. I knew I was innocent. There was no evidence, no phone call, no note, no trace of wrongdoing. My mother hadn't brought drugs. The whole thing was a misunderstanding, born from a guard's inappropriate behavior and my mother's courage to speak up.

Even the officer-judge admitted it.

"There's really no proof that you were going to receive drugs from your mom," he said with a shrug, "but we're going to write you up anyway."

He didn't even pretend it was fair.

That single write-up, despite the lack of evidence, shot my classification points through the roof, and those points are everything in prison. They determine your privileges, but they also determine where you go. As a result, I was transferred to one of the worst prisons in the state of Colorado: Buena Vista Correctional Facility, which prisoners nicknamed "Bew-nee."

RIOT IN THE HOLE

Buena Vista is located in the same facility as the boot camp program, so the same town where I had completed boot camp now became the place of my punishment. They had three levels or prison there: the boot camp, the minimum-restrictive side, and the maximum-security unit where I was headed. Buena Vista had a reputation as one of the most dangerous facilities in the state. It was known throughout Colorado's prison system as "Gladiator School."

I knew what was coming wouldn't be easy. They shackled me and put me on the transport bus. I arrived at Buena Vista and was thrown directly into the hole again, but this time, it was darker and even more miserable.

I had only been there two days when I heard the whispers. Inmates yelling through the vents, "We're going to riot tomorrow. Get ready."

My heart sank. *God, what did I walk into?* I didn't want any part of this, but I also knew that when a riot breaks out in the hole, it doesn't matter if you're innocent. It doesn't matter what side you're on. You're in it.

The next morning, it started. Inmates flooded their cells. They started throwing things—books, trash, trays, even feces—out into the hallway. It was total chaos.

The guards responded the way they always do when control slips: with overwhelming force. They came down the corridor with OC spray, a tear gas so strong it makes regular pepper spray feel like cologne. One by one, they gassed every single cell.

I wasn't involved in the riot. I was reading my Bible and hadn't even spoken to anyone, but innocence doesn't buy you much in that place. I heard the gas coming before I felt it, heard the screams first, inmates coughing, gagging, and crying out in pain. The hiss of the canisters. The shouts of officers.

It came closer. Closer. Closer. Finally, it reached my door.

The moment it hit, I began choking. My throat clenched shut. My eyes started pouring. My skin burned. I tried to suck in a breath, but the gas seared my lungs. I dropped to the floor, gagging, trying not to panic, trying to pray, but even prayer felt suffocated by the pain.

I curled up, clutching the Bible I'd been reading. The same hands that had turned its pages now trembled uncontrollably.

God, why am I here?

There was no answer. Just the sound of coughing, screaming, steel doors—then silence.

Yet even in that moment, somewhere in the center of the agony, I knew God was with me. I didn't feel it the way I had during worship services or revival meetings. I didn't hear His voice, but something in me held on. That quiet thread of faith that says, *Even now, I will not let go.*

I remember lying under that thin prison-issued blanket, trying to catch my breath. My lungs were still raw from the gas, my eyes burning, my skin stinging. I had my face buried in the crook of my arm, whispering prayers between coughing fits.

What did I get myself into? I kept asking.

Eventually, the storm passed. I stumbled to the sink, splashing cold water on my face, trying to wash away the chemical residue and the sense of disbelief. Everything started to settle, and I could breathe again, at least physically.

Three weeks later, they pulled me out of the hole and sent me to the general intake pod. If I thought the gas chamber of solitary confinement was bad, I had no idea what was waiting for me.

GLADIATOR SCHOOL

The intake pod had earned its name: Gladiator School. As soon as the doors opened, people started fighting. When the doors closed, people started fighting. If someone took too long in the shower, it was another fight. If you looked at someone the wrong way—fight. It was relentless.

Right away, I hit my knees in that cell and started praying hard. *God, I need your protection in this place. I don't know why I'm here, but You do. Show me.*

To my amazement, He did.

Looking back now, I realize that the raw chaos of Buena Vista was God's tool to bring me back to Him. I'd grown jaded in Delta and Colorado Springs. I was angry, spiritually numb. I hadn't walked away from my faith, but I wasn't walking in it fully either. So God, in His mercy, threw me into the fire.

In that hellish place, I met some men who, by every worldly standard, should've been broken. They were lifers, men who weren't ever going home: murderers, multiple offenders, men with crimes so dark they didn't even bother hoping for parole. But some of them—*some of them*—had met Jesus, and those guys were more free than most people I knew on the outside.

It rocked me. These were men who had lost everything, yet they carried joy, peace, and purpose. They were worshiping and encouraging each other, and through their witness, God began to heal my heart. My bitterness started to crack, and my jadedness started to fall away. God used lifers to restore my faith.

Still, that prison was brutal. We were on a twenty-two-hour lockdown schedule, which meant you were locked in your cell twenty-two hours a day. If you wanted more time out, you had to get a job. I applied to work in the kitchen, and thankfully, I was accepted. It was tough work, but it got me out of the cell more often, and in that place, extra time out of your cell was a gift.

The rules were strict, often unspoken, and enforced by inmates as well guards. Everything was racially segregated. Whites stayed with whites. Blacks with blacks. Latinos with Latinos. The only exception was if you were gang-affiliated and had permission to mix. But for some reason, if you were a Christian, those rules didn't seem to apply.

I sat with people from every race and background, and I wasn't confronted or threatened. Being a follower of Jesus put me in a category all my own and placed a bubble of favor around me.

There were exceptions to this. For example, when it came time to shower, everyone was in danger. You needed a shower buddy to stand guard for you while you showered because ambushes happened in those moments. It was one of the most vulnerable places to be. My cellmate and I had a system: I would shower while he stood guard, fully clothed, watching the door like a hawk. When I finished, I'd dry off, get dressed, lace up my boots, and do the same for him. It was a ritual of survival.

Buena Vista was a crazy place full of violence and volatility, but strangely, I felt God's presence and favor like never before. I didn't get into fights, and no one harassed me. On the contrary, I was able to form some real friendships, even across racial lines. Somehow, in a prison that should've devoured me, I stood untouched. It made no sense, except for God.

A year passed in that crazy place, and slowly—mercifully—my points dropped again. This time, they dropped low enough to qualify me for a minimum-restrictive facility. I could finally leave Buena Vista's maximum-security side behind.

I was ecstatic. *Get me out of this hellhole,* I thought. *Anywhere but here.*

They transferred me to the minimum side of the same facility, but it felt like a whole new world. It was calmer and safer. The tension that filled the max unit finally lifted, and not long after arriving, I got approved for something I had dreamed of for years: work program!

STEPS TOWARD FREEDOM

After four and a half years behind concrete and razor wire, I finally stepped outside the prison walls to work in the community. I still wore the orange jumpsuit, but for the first time in years, I tasted something that felt like freedom. It was glorious.

We'd get driven into town and take on labor jobs—nothing fancy, just regular work, but to me, it was sacred. I loved every errand, every building I entered, every tree I passed. I could feel the sky above me again. I could smell the world outside the gates.

That season helped restore something deep in me. I started going back to church services regularly. I led Bible studies again and prayed with other inmates. I encouraged guys who had lost their way. It was like the calling God put in me all those years ago was rekindled in full flame. Hope had returned, and with it, a deep sense of purpose.

Unfortunately, just before the end, I faced another crushing setback. I was denied parole. Again. Denied the halfway house. *Again.* Disappointment washed over me, though it was becoming a familiar feeling. I started questioning everything again.

Eventually, my points dropped once more, and I was transferred to my final stop: Rifle Correctional Facility. While there, my new cellmate gave me a strange piece of advice. I was telling him about the disappointment of being denied parole and halfway house. That's when he said, "Why don't you try Fort Collins? They accept anybody up there."

I didn't know a soul in Fort Collins. It was about forty-five minutes north of where I'd grown up, but I had no connections there, no job lined up, and no place to stay. Still, what did I have to lose? So I told my caseworker, "Next time I apply, I want to request Fort Collins."

And wouldn't you know it, I got accepted. Five years into my sentence—five years of confinement, transfers, ministry, riots, restoration, heartbreak, and hope—I was finally approved for a halfway house.

It's hard to describe the flood of emotions. Joy. Gratitude. Disbelief. Fear. Nervous excitement. It felt like my soul was stretching into a new skin.

Five years is a long time no matter what, but behind bars, five years feels like a lifetime. Finally, after a lifetime, I was getting out. I didn't know what to expect. I didn't know who I would call. I didn't know where I would go. I had no plan or community. All I knew for sure was that, as soon as I got out, the first thing I was going to do was find a church and plug in with everything I had.

Whatever came next, I wasn't going to walk into it alone. God had carried me this far, and I wanted to stick with Him into the future.

CHAPTER EIGHT

STARTING FROM SCRATCH

NO MATTER HOW MUCH PROGRESS I MADE, I COULDN'T shake the feeling that, somehow, the ladder would be yanked out from under me again. It had happened to me too many times by this point. Just when things seemed stable, the bottom would drop out. So I expected it to happen again.

From the prison in Rifle, I was transported to a holding facility in Cañon City. That's where they staged us before our release. It was supposed to be a brief stop, a transition, but for me, the wait stretched on. One day became two, then seven, then eight. Each morning, they would call out names for those being released, and each morning, my name wasn't on the list.

By the ninth day, I had nearly given up hope. My mind was a battlefield of worst-case scenarios: *Maybe there was a mistake. Maybe I wasn't actually approved. Maybe this was just another false start.*

And then, finally, they called my name.

It's hard to describe the relief that hit me at that moment. I felt like I could breathe for the first time in years. They took me to the back and handed me a set of street clothes—a wrinkled blue polo shirt, brown khakis, and a pair of stiff black dress shoes. Not exactly stylish, but to me, they were the garments of freedom. They gave me an inmate ID, my last tether to the past five and a half years, and loaded me onto the van bound for Denver.

That drive was quiet and *long*. I stared out the window, wondering what life would be like on the other side. What would it be like to walk into a grocery store again, to smell real soap, to use a phone without bars around me? I didn't have answers, only questions and hope.

At the halfway house in Fort Collins, they checked me in, gave me a brief orientation, and assigned me to a bunk. A few hours later, my mom showed up. She brought me a box containing multiple pairs of shoes and bottles of cologne. That was all I had to my name, but I'll tell you, after five and a half years of state-issued everything, spraying that cologne on my neck made me feel more human than I had in a long time. I couldn't stop smelling my own shirt.

God had his hand on me—I know that now, and I knew it then. By the time I got to the halfway house, I already had a job lined up. A woman my mom knew had offered me work at a place called Streamside on Fall River, a beautiful lodge tucked away in the mountains of Estes Park, and I was eager to get started. The commute from Fort Collins to Estes was forty-five minutes each way, and without a car, that was no small hurdle. I was willing to figure it out.

The halfway house didn't let me start working immediately. Their process is structured, and for good reason. When you enter, you're placed on Level One. That meant no job yet—just orientation, paperwork, and reacclimation—but there was one thing I *was* allowed to do: find a church.

That was nonnegotiable for me. I knew, deep in my bones, that the only way I was going to stay grounded was by being rooted in a community of faith. Not just for accountability, though that mattered, but for relationship and spiritual protection.

I visited a few churches, but when I walked into Vineyard Church of the Rockies, something clicked. It wasn't flashy or big, but it was *real*. The people welcomed me, not with suspicion but with open arms. I started connecting with the young adult ministry, building friendships that, by the grace of God, still exist today.

REBUILDING A LIFE

Those early days were fragile. I was rebuilding a life, yes, but also rediscovering who I was. I was no longer the street kid, the drug dealer, or the inmate. I was becoming something new, something better.

My new friends not only invited me to their Bible studies, they gave me rides to church, prayed with me, and included me in their lives. For someone who had spent years being watched, searched, and distrusted, it meant everything to be seen as a person again and treated as someone worth investing in.

Looking back now, I believe God orchestrated the whole thing. I had applied to multiple halfway houses in Denver and had been rejected, but the one that said yes was up in Fort Collins, far away from the people and places that had dragged me down. That gave me a real chance at a clean slate and a fresh start. I don't believe it was a coincidence.

Still, adjusting to freedom proved to be harder than I expected. It felt like I had been dropped into a world that had moved on without me. It was a lot faster and louder than I remembered. This hit me hard the first time I left the halfway house on a three-hour pass. My mom picked me up and took me to Walmart so I could buy a few essentials. Seemed simple enough, but the moment we stepped through those sliding glass doors, my senses were assaulted. Everything was just too much.

The colors overwhelmed me: neon packaging, fluorescent lighting, walls bursting with signs and sales and screaming reds and yellows. After years of living in the dull monochrome of prison, surrounded by white walls, green inmate uniforms, blue security shirts, gray steel, and cement, my eyes weren't ready. I felt like I was tripping. And then came the people. They were all rushing past, brushing my shoulder without a word, cutting across aisles, carts swerving, their kids screaming. It was overstimulating in a way I never could have anticipated.

In prison, there are unspoken rules of respect. You never stand too close, you always acknowledge someone's space, and you don't step behind a man unless you're in a line. There's a strange kind of order behind bars, a quiet awareness of proximity and personal space, but here, on the outside, no one made eye contact, no one said "excuse me." Everyone was rushing.

Within minutes, I was having a full-blown panic attack. My heart pounded, and my vision narrowed. I grabbed my mom's hand and whispered, "I need to leave. I can't do this." We left the cart right there with everything in it and walked out of the store.

That's when I realized I had been mentally and emotionally institutionalized. I had been conditioned to ask permission for everything, to live by a schedule someone else created, to keep my head down and stay in my lane, and now, out in the world, without those boundaries, I felt exposed. I felt like I was doing something wrong just by being outside.

That feeling stuck with me. For weeks, maybe months, every time I stepped out of the halfway house, I felt like I was being watched. I kept waiting for someone to tell me I had messed up, to slam the door behind me and say, "Just kidding—you're going back." It wasn't until I finally got off parole that I felt like I could breathe again. That I could actually live.

When I was approved to start working, I had that job waiting for me in Estes Park. My mom's friend Julie, who was the manager at a resort, hooked it up for me. She was a godsend, gave me a chance and hired me fresh out of prison. She was the first to believe in me, and I'm forever grateful for that. Working in

Estes was a huge blessing, no doubt, but I was in Fort Collins, and Estes Park was a forty-five-minute drive up winding mountain roads. I had no car and no license, so I didn't know how to get there. However, I was determined to figure it out. I told myself, *Do whatever it takes. No excuses. This is your second chance. Don't waste it.*

At first, my mom helped. She would drive up from Denver, pick me up in Fort Collins, take me to Estes, and then do the return trip—all in one day. That's a two-hour drive *each way*. She did it as long as she could, but eventually, it was too much. I didn't blame her.

So I mapped out a route for myself. It required me to wake up at 3:00 a.m. every morning and ride my bike through the cold and dark to the bus stop in downtown Fort Collins. From there, I caught a bus south to Loveland. Then, I would switch to another bus that dropped me off at an old Kmart on Highway 34. Finally, from there, I carpooled with two other guys and headed up the mountain. They worked at a business near mine, and they agreed to let me stash another bike behind the building. Once we arrived in Estes Park, I would hop on that bike and pedal uphill to my job.

At the end of the day, I did it all in reverse. Twelve to fifteen hours a day, just to work and keep moving forward, but I didn't complain, and I didn't get bitter. After all, I was free, and I was building a new life for myself.

That season was a crucible. Then again, it felt like a privilege. Not everyone gets another chance, and I wasn't going to waste mine.

THE WINK, THE WORD, AND THE WOMAN

I was out of prison, back in the community, and trying to figure out what life looked like now that the bars were behind me. In many ways, I was still learning how to live free, but I was okay with that. For the first time in years, I had hope that maybe God could still use me.

What I didn't expect was how quickly things would progress, both in my job and in the church. I threw myself into everything they offered: Bible studies, volunteer opportunities, community nights. I showed up early, stayed late, and built friendships rooted in faith instead of addiction. It wasn't long before I was trusted with real responsibility.

They made me the head usher for the young adult service and later gave me leadership over the hospitality team. Leadership always seemed to follow me wherever I went, and after recommitting my life to Jesus, those moments of stepping up started to feel more like stepping into something I was built for. Funny thing was, I was still wearing an ankle monitor at the time. Yet there I was, trusted with the tithe money. Only God could write that kind of story: an ankle monitor under my slacks but an offering bucket in my hand.

That's when I met Lacey. It was a Sunday like any other. I was standing at the sanctuary doors handing out service sheets to people as they walked in. It was part of my role, but it was more than that—it was my way of creating space for people to feel welcome and seen. That day, Lacey showed up as a volunteer to help. She stood beside me, smiling, and something stirred in me. I don't mean fireworks or violins—nothing dramatic. Just a thought: *She might be the one.*

Now, let me be clear—I wasn't *that* guy. You know the type. The overly eager, spiritually manipulative kind who walks up to a woman and says, "The Lord told me you're my wife." No, I kept that thought to myself. I just handed out bulletins and tried not to sound like a nervous teenager every time we talked.

Lacey, on the other hand, didn't waste time with small talk. She looked me square in the eyes and said, "I'm in sober living. I used to be a heroin addict. Just got out of rehab."

She said it like a fact, not a confession. There was no shame in her tone, just honesty, so I matched her vulnerability.

"Well," I said, "I'm in the halfway house."

That was it. We had no filters. We were just two broken people standing side by side in the house of God, each holding a past they no longer wanted to live in. Strangely enough, it felt right. Our stories fit together like pieces of the same puzzle. She wasn't afraid of where I'd been, and I wasn't afraid of where she'd come from.

But then she disappeared. The next Sunday, she didn't show up at church. Or the Sunday after that. In fact, a whole month passed. Then two. I figured she'd relapsed. That was the world we came from. People vanished all the time, so I didn't dwell on it. I stayed the course—worked my program, served in the church, and tried to keep my head down. Life was moving forward.

Eventually, I started dating a girl I met online, but I didn't feel any spark with her the way I had with Lacey. She wasn't a believer. It was a relationship built on convenience, not covenant. We soon began sleeping together, though I knew deep down I was living in compromise. I was trying to walk the line, to live a new life with one foot still planted in the old one.

Then came the Sunday that would shake me to my core. Pastor Rick Olmstead, the founding pastor of Vineyard Church of the Rockies, stood up at the end of service and said something that would ultimately change the course of my life: "I really feel like there's someone here in a relationship you're not supposed to be in. God is telling you—it's time to let it go."

I went cold. There was no way he could've known. The girl I was dating didn't go to our church. No one knew I was seeing her, but at that moment, I knew God was talking to me. Yet I didn't end it. You would've thought I learned my lesson the first time God told me to break up with a girl I was dating. However, I didn't put two and two together at that moment. Instead, I went home, shrugged it off, and kept going like nothing happened.

Then came the next Sunday. Same pastor. Same tone. "I still feel like someone here hasn't listened. That relationship is not from God. You need to walk away now."

This time the fear of God hit me hard, and I couldn't shake it. I called the girl and gave her one of the worst breakup lines in history. "Hey, my pastor said I'm not supposed to be with you, so we need to break up."

Not smooth. Not kind. But at least it was done.

Funny enough, we're friends now on Facebook. She's married, seems happy, and we even comment on each other's posts occasionally, but our relationship never would've worked out. She didn't want kids and had no interest in faith. I was trying to force something that didn't fit.

Around the same time, I'd started browsing Christian Mingle, that dating site with the cheesiest commercials and the sincerest intentions. I wasn't trying to force anything, just scrolling, but nothing clicked. It all felt like filler, like I was trying to fill a void that couldn't be filled with profile bios and filtered pictures.

I was scrolling through profiles one night, bored, curious, and probably a little desperate. I was broke, still in the halfway house, and the only thing you could do for free was wink at people and hope for the best. Paying to send messages wasn't an option, but I figured if I saw someone I recognized, I could always just strike up a conversation at church.

And then, one day, Lacey's face popped up on my screen on Christian Mingle. After months of not seeing her, suddenly here she was again, not in the church foyer, but in my feed. I hit the "wink" button.

The very next Sunday, she walked through the church doors again for the first time in months. I was standing in the same place we'd met, handing out service sheets at the door, when she walked in. Her eyes locked on mine like a lioness who had already made up her mind on her prey.

Again, she didn't bother with small talk. "Where are you sitting?" she asked.

"In my normal spot," I replied, trying to act cooler than I felt.

"Well, I'm sitting with you today."

I stood there stunned. No woman had ever pursued me like that. I felt like a little kid. My voice might've cracked when I said, "Okay."

We sat together during worship, and afterward, she didn't leave my side. I was trying to finish up tasks, talking to people, and there she was—lingering, present, relentless in the gentlest way.

I remember thinking, *Maybe she wants me to ask her out.* So I did.

"Would you want to grab a coffee sometime?"

She smiled. "No, but I would like some ice cream."

That night we went out for ice cream at a place in Fort Collins called Walrus Ice Cream, and the rest, as they say, is history. It wasn't long before I realized she was the one. There was something different about her. We didn't just share similar pasts, we shared the same vision of the future. We both knew what it meant to fall apart, but more importantly, we knew what it meant to start over.

This August, we'll celebrate thirteen years of marriage, and it all started with a wink, a word from God, and a woman who had no time for small talk.

A BIG, BOLD YES

Finding Lacey was the kind of quiet miracle that sneaks up on you. In terms of our upbringing, we came from completely different worlds. Her childhood was comfortable, affluent, and structured, and mine was anything but. Yet somehow, we met right where it mattered most: on the road of faith and recovery. We were scarred by different pasts but healing in the same direction, and we bonded over our sobriety and hunger for something better.

Lacey was nine months older than me, and we had enough common ground to make the cultural gaps feel like footnotes. There was harmony between us. We didn't fight—not then, and honestly, not much now. Thirteen years in, I can count our arguments on one hand. Most couples would kill for that kind of peace.

Eight months after we met, I left the halfway house, though I was still on a tether, with a state-issued ankle bracelet that reminded me daily of where I stood. They call it "non-res" (for "nonresident"). You're still considered an inmate, but you live outside the facility.

By then, I'd been working at Streamside in Estes Park for a while. Curt, the owner, took a chance on me when most wouldn't, and in doing so, he gave me more than a job. He also gave me dignity. Curt even offered me a loan for my first car, let me move into a tiny studio apartment on the property, and eventually promoted me to head of maintenance. The lodge had twenty-two units, twenty acres of forest, hot tubs, pipes, plows, and landscaping, and I was responsible for all of it.

It wasn't glamorous, but it was mine. After years of living inside fences, even a three-hundred-square-foot studio with creaky floors felt like a castle. I still had to call in to my parole officer every night, blow into a breathalyzer, and report for random check-ins, but I was out. I could walk to the gym. I could walk under the stars. I could plan a life, and I had someone to plan it with.

Lacey and I knew marriage was coming. We talked about it often, whispered about it between Sunday services and late-night phone calls, but I wanted to do it right. To earn money for an engagement ring, I picked up odd jobs, saved every spare dollar, and did side work fixing pipes and painting trim.

By February 2011, I had it. That Sunday, I pulled our pastor, David Brooks, aside and shared my plan. I consider him one of my best friends, a close mentor, and still one of my pastors. I wanted to propose during the service. Though I was terrified of public speaking, I knew this was the kind of moment worth risking everything on. I asked Lacey to come help me "with announcements," and she, totally unsuspecting, agreed.

When it came time to speak, I stood on the stage in front of about three hundred people, heart pounding. I made it through the announcements, then I turned to her, dropped to one knee, and asked her to marry me.

The room erupted in cheers, applause, and even a few tears. Before I could finish the gesture, Lacey snatched the ring out of my hand and slid it onto her finger with a big, bold, "Yes." There's a video of it on YouTube.[3] If you watch closely, you'll see how fast she moves. She didn't wait. She knew.

We didn't want a long engagement, and there was no point in waiting. Life moves fast, and after everything we'd come through, we weren't about to waste time playing it slow. We set the date at August 11, 2012. The halfway house approved it, and the state said yes.

So we got married.

Even now, it's hard to describe the collision of emotions I felt walking down the aisle. It was equal parts fear and joy, redemption and disbelief. Here I was, not long out of prison, still wearing an ankle bracelet beneath my dress pants, yet stepping into one of the holiest, most hope-filled moments of my life. The truth is, I felt like I had a lot of catching up to do. I'd gone into prison at twenty-one and was released just shy of twenty-seven. I'd lost most of my twenties to cement walls and cold chow lines.

We invited everyone. More than two hundred guests showed up to celebrate and witness something that felt impossible just a few years earlier. One of the pastors from Vineyard Church

---

3   Lacey Scadden, "Rick and Lacey Wedding Proposal," YouTube video, 0:59, February 29, 2012, https://www.youtube.com/watch?v=L-WMVcY34JU.

officiated the ceremony. I remember standing at the altar, ankle bracelet discreetly hidden, as he began to speak blessings over us, but then he said something curious.

He started talking about twins. He said something like, "When the twins are up crying in the middle of the night, you two will really need to work together as a team." It caught me off guard. Twins? We hadn't told anyone about any plans for kids, let alone multiples. Lacey and I exchanged glances. We smiled, but the words stuck with us. At the time, we chalked it up to a metaphor—or maybe just a pastor caught up in the poetry of the moment. However, those words would prove to be prophetic.

We didn't have a honeymoon. Lacey had just accepted a teaching job, and the school year started that Monday. Instead of jetting off to a beach somewhere, we stayed home, made a meal, and launched straight into real life.

That first year of marriage wasn't easy. In fact, it was pretty tough. Not because we didn't love each other—we did, deeply—but because our lives had come from two totally different worlds. She was an only child raised in an affluent, orderly home. I came from poverty, one of six kids, raised in mess and noise. Where she had quiet, I had tension. Where she had structure, I had the streets. Our habits, expectations, and ways of doing even the smallest things collided under one roof.

In her house, you folded towels a certain way. In my house, you were just glad to have clean ones. In her world, you made a grocery list and stuck to it. In mine, you made dinner with whatever you had—creativity over consistency. These weren't just differences. They were lived-in ways of being, and in that first year, we had to sort through all of them.

But we talked, and we prayed, and we wrestled through it. No matter how hard it was, we knew this marriage was built on something deeper than compatibility—it was built on covenant—and that kind of bond can hold up under the weight of any baggage you bring into it.

DOUBLE BLESSINGS, DOUBLE RECKONINGS

Three months into our marriage, Lacey and I got the news that she was pregnant.

Excitement surged through us at the thought of becoming parents, but fear quickly followed. We were young, just trying to find our footing. I was still commuting to Estes Park for work, and as a first-year teacher, Lacey was stretched thin in every direction. We lived in a modest two-bedroom apartment in Loveland, barely making ends meet, so the idea of raising a child, though beautiful, was daunting.

I remember praying before the first ultrasound, "God, please let the heartbeat be strong. Let this baby be healthy." Deep down, I harbored the typical fears of a first-time parent: *What if our child had a serious medical condition? Would I be strong enough? Would I know how to love through that?*

The day of the heartbeat appointment came, and the sound was strong and clear. Relief swept over us. We laughed, hugged, and imagined our future. I was convinced it would be a boy, but that wasn't the last surprise in store.

Weeks later, we returned for the twenty-week ultrasound. I tried to read the black-and-white blur on the screen, but it was all shapes and shadows to me. Then the technician paused, drew in a breath, and said, "Oh! I have a surprise for you. There are two heads."

My face must have gone pale. My heart froze. I stammered, stunned, "What do you mean two heads? A two-headed baby monster? What is happening?"

She quickly corrected herself. "No, no, I'm so sorry. You're having twins!"

The panic turned into a flood of mixed emotion—relief, wonder, terror, awe. *Twins?* And then, like a flash of divine déjà vu, I remembered the pastor who had officiated our wedding just a few months earlier. During the ceremony, he had spoken about twins, about us needing to lean on each other when "the twins are crying in the middle of the night." At the time, I thought it was metaphorical, or maybe just an odd tangent. Now, I knew it had been a word from God—a prophetic blessing, spoken before we even knew it would come to pass.

We left the clinic in a daze. That night, we cancelled the plans we'd made for a one-year anniversary getaway. Instead, we drove to the store and bought two cribs.

From that moment on, everything doubled: twice the diapers, twice the bottles, twice the financial stress, and, thank God, twice the joy. But even that joy wasn't without its complications.

A few days later, Lacey's parents called and said, "We've decided to sell our properties and move to Loveland to help raise these babies." Then her father made a staggering offer: "Find us a house and one for yourselves. We'll buy both. You can rent from us and pay what you can afford." I was floored. This was my first encounter with real generosity from a family of wealth.

We found a house and moved in. It should've been a season of peace and preparation, but I was hiding a secret that threatened to unravel everything good in my life. You see, back in Estes Park, before Lacey and I got married, I had formed a troubling relationship with one of the housekeepers at the resort where I worked. It began as flirting but escalated quickly into something physical. We never had sex, but we went right to the edge. I told myself I would stop once I got married, but I didn't. The emotional affair continued even after we exchanged vows.

One afternoon, we were alone, and it almost went too far. But in a moment of clarity, I pulled away and said, "We have to stop this." I walked out, shaken by how close I'd come to ruining everything.

That night, I knew I had to confess. The guilt was eating me alive. In my family, infidelity was a familiar plague that ran generations deep. It was a pattern I swore I'd never repeat, but here I was, tangled up in it just the same.

Telling Lacey was the hardest thing I've ever done. She was

pregnant with our twins. We had just moved into our new home, and I had to look her in the eyes and admit that I had nearly destroyed our marriage before it really began.

She was devastated. Rightfully so. I sought counsel from Pastor David, who walked me through the storm with grace and truth. He stood by me, even when I didn't deserve it. Together, we made a plan: I would quit my job in Estes Park, I would set firm boundaries, and I would take full responsibility.

When I told my boss what happened, he agreed to help put safeguards in place while I searched for a new job. Trust, once broken, doesn't rebuild overnight, but Lacey and I committed to the long road of restoration. Honestly, I'm such a lucky man. Lacey forgave me and chose to stick with me. I remember the sting of what Kelly had done to me, and now here I was, doing the same thing to someone else. It hit me hard. I was full of shame. But Lacey's response, her love and forgiveness, was something I had never experienced before. That kind of grace gave me permission to finally change my ways.

Looking back, I see that season as a divine breaking point. God didn't just bless us with two children; he also exposed the parts of me that still needed to die—chiefly my pride and my secrecy. All that generational baggage had to be cast aside completely.

TINY CRIBS, BIG BEGINNINGS

We were young, in love, and excited to be building a family. Then came another complication. Lacey was diagnosed with preeclampsia and put on bed rest. Everything slowed down, and every day became a cautious countdown. Then one evening, as we were preparing to go out for dinner—a rare treat in those days—she stood up and her water broke.

As first-time parents, we didn't recognize the signs immediately. The twins weren't due for six more weeks, but when she called the doctor, his urgency was clear: "Get to the hospital. Now."

And so, the twins arrived six weeks early on June 6, 2013. Sadie came first. Tiny but strong, her cry was immediate. Her lungs definitely worked. It was a relief we couldn't fully put into words.

Then came Amariah. From the start, she resisted. She wasn't ready, and when she arrived, she wasn't breathing. Her skin was blue, her body limp, and for five of the longest minutes of my life, there was no sound in the room—only the quiet, focused intensity of the medical team working over her tiny form.

Lacey and I held our breath. Panic clawed at our chests, but the doctors didn't waver. They performed a procedure, introducing fluid into her lungs to force them open. Then, suddenly, the silence shattered—her first breath followed by a cry. It was a sound I will never forget. Life had arrived, and it arrived in stereo.

Both girls were so small that their heads barely filled the palm of my hand, but they were alive. Even though they were healthy, they were still too young to feed on their own, so the NICU became our home for the next month. We lived in the hum of machines and the beep of monitors. The nurses taught us how to change diapers, feed bottles, and care for our preemie girls. What could have been a frightening season became a gift. The NICU taught us how to be parents.

In the midst of all that joy and stress, I was dealing with another major change: I had quit my job in Estes Park and launched my own painting business. I knew the trade. Heck, I had grown up on ladders and drop cloths, working with my dad. It felt like coming full circle, but this time, I was the boss.

That first year as a business owner was brutal. Anyone who's launched a business from scratch knows the grind of quoting jobs, hiring help, managing clients, keeping books, doing the work yourself when help falls through. There were late nights, early mornings, and more than one moment when I thought, *What am I doing?*

Still, it eventually paid off. I made more money that first year than I had in several years of working for someone else, though it came at a cost—chiefly exhaustion, time away from my family, and emotional strain. To help fill in the gaps, I reached out to a local painting company, M&E Painting, owned by a guy named Matt Shoup. I had seen his face on benches around town, and something told me to reach out. They were hiring subcontractors, so I applied. It was supposed to be a group interview, but I was the only one who showed up.

I told them my story. Well, I told them *part* of my story. I left out the prison years. Still, it was enough. They brought me on.

As summer wound down, Matt posted something online about hiring for leadership roles. I was intrigued. The company was growing, and I had leadership experience. Not long after that post, Matt and I found ourselves on a job site together. The client was a lawyer—a particularly angry one. She'd had a bad experience with a previous crew, and now she was furious. I was sent in to fix it. Matt showed up to support. She was shouting, we were sweating, and all I could do was focus on getting it right.

That job was pivotal. It gave Matt a firsthand look at how I handled pressure, confrontation, and responsibility.

At home, life was no less intense. With two newborns, a recovering wife, a new house, and a new business, there came the deep weariness of a man still learning how to stay whole. There was joy, yes. Unspeakable joy. But there were also shadows— parts of me I thought I had buried, still clawing to the surface. It would take more than a business, a marriage, or even the joy of fatherhood to heal those wounds.

And yet, through all of it, I could feel the grace of God pressing in. I wasn't just learning how to be a father, or a husband, or a businessman. I was learning how to be a man redeemed.

A WHOLE NEW CHAPTER

The same morning that we stood in front of the angry lawyer's house, I finally worked up the courage to tell Matt the whole truth. I had been subcontracting with his company for a while now—grateful for the work, grateful for the chance to build a new life, but deep down, I knew I was living in two worlds again. I wasn't hiding sin, but I hadn't yet shared the full story of where I'd come from. He had taken a chance on me, and he deserved to know everything, come what may.

So I looked Matt in the eye and said, "Hey, there's something you need to know about me. I've actually been to prison."

His reaction surprised me. "Oh," he said with curiosity, not judgment. "Well, we definitely need to hear that story."

And that's exactly what happened. The following week, we sat down, and I laid it all out: the addiction, the betrayal, the wreck, the sentence, the climb out. I didn't sugarcoat anything. I just told him the truth.

That conversation changed our relationship dynamic, though in a positive way. Matt saw something in me that I hadn't fully seen in myself, and he didn't treat my past as a liability. In the weeks that followed, he and his wife, Emily, invited us to dinner, and he offered me a job. They came alongside Lacey and me as friends, mentors, and encouragers.

To this day Matt and I are still really good friends. A lot of who I am today I owe to him. He has challenged me in ways that caused me to grow as a man, a husband, a leader, a speaker, and now an author. He has been my biggest encouragement in writing this book. Matt, if you're reading this, "Thank you."

Within a few months, I was promoted to senior project manager, a position that gave me not just responsibility but dignity. It was a lesson I would carry forward for the rest of my life: *Testimony is currency.* When you tell your story, it creates space for the grace of God.

By now, I was experiencing more freedom than I had in years.

I'd been released from the ankle monitor and had no more halfway house check-ins or curfews. I was officially on parole. That may not sound like a milestone to some, but to me, it felt like I had crossed a great invisible threshold. I was still under supervision—five years of it, technically—but the physical weight of confinement was gone. I could breathe a little easier.

Still, I never forgot the fragility of it all. Every month, I had to report to the Department of Corrections office in Fort Collins, and every time I stepped into that building, a chill would run through me. Even if I hadn't done anything wrong, even if I was following every rule, I couldn't shake the fear that they might arrest me anyway. That they would find some issue, revoke my parole, and send me back. That fear, the sense that the ladder could be kicked out from under me at any moment, never really left.

Despite the fear, life was good. Working with Matt, I was earning more than I ever had before. I was growing, not just financially but personally. He was teaching me leadership, business, and most of all, how to live with integrity on the other side of a broken past.

My marriage, too, was stabilizing. Lacey and I had weathered many storms, but we made a decision together that divorce would never be on the table. Whatever came, we would face it together. Out of that resolve came some practical boundaries and rules I live by to this day. I don't text another woman unless my wife is included. I don't meet one-on-one with another woman, especially behind closed doors. I don't ride in a car with a woman I don't know, and if I do have to be in a meeting, I text Lacey ahead of time and let her know exactly what's going on.

These boundaries don't come from insecurity. They come from wisdom. I know where I've been, I know the generational patterns I've inherited, and I refuse to repeat them any longer. I choose to break the cycle.

Our marriage wasn't perfect then, but it was strong because

it had been tested. We had chosen the hard path of healing and invited God into the process every step of the way. Honestly, I was living a life I never thought possible, with a stable home, a healthy marriage, two beautiful daughters, a career that gave me purpose, and a community that believed in me. Most of all, I was walking in the calling that had been on my life since the beginning.

I believe that season shaped us into the couple we are today. The safeguards and boundaries we put in place have kept us both safe from making the same mistakes. Life is like that sometimes. It's often the hard things that shape us the most.

Just ahead, God had another divine connection waiting. A connection that would take the pieces of my past and position them for kingdom purpose, because nothing is wasted—not even the prison years.

FULL CIRCLE GRACE

Sometimes, even in a season of strength, God whispers that it's time to move.

At Vineyard Church of the Rockies, where Lacey and I had both poured ourselves into ministry—her in the children's department and me overseeing men's groups and leadership initiatives—we began to feel a quiet sense that our season was coming to a close. It was nothing dramatic. There was no offense or scandal, just a holy unease. The atmosphere had changed. The services didn't resonate like they once had. Decisions were being made in leadership that we couldn't fully support.

Still, we weren't going to leave bitter or prematurely. One of the best pieces of wisdom I ever received was this: *Leave well.* If you're going to close a door, close it with peace. So we stayed and waited for clarity.

And then one afternoon, my phone rang. It was my brother.

"Hey, do you remember that church we went to as teenagers—Center Point?"

Of course I did. That was the church where I had first heard the gospel and the place where Pastor Mark prophesied over my life that I would be a pastor one day. To me, Center Point was sacred ground, even if it had faded into memory during my years in prison.

"Well," my brother said, "do you remember Aaron from youth group? He's a pastor now. He married Pastor Mark's daughter, Becky, and they just planted a new church in Loveland. It's called Citipointe."

The second he said it, something inside me lit up. I turned to Lacey and said, "We need to check this church out."

The next Sunday, we fulfilled our responsibilities at Vineyard's early service. Then we slipped out, drove across town, and walked into Citipointe's second service. It was held in a beat-up, one-way-in, one-way-out warehouse with stained carpet and makeshift everything. Yet, the presence of God was so thick in the room, it stopped me in my tracks.

As worship began, I collapsed into a seat and started to weep. It was an ugly cry, the kind where snot and tears become indistinguishable. I couldn't explain it, and I hadn't expected it, but God met me there in that forgotten corner of a warehouse sanctuary and reminded me of everything I didn't know I had lost.

I hadn't realized it, but my heart had grown numb in the routine. The past two years at Vineyard had been marked by faithful attendance but spiritual flatness. I had been moving but not growing. Showing up but not encountering. And this moment of unfiltered worship was like a defibrillator to my soul.

I didn't talk to Pastor Aaron or Becky that day. I just left undone.

Lacey and I prayed that night. "God, what are You saying?"

The next Sunday, we went back to Vineyard out of obedience, but it didn't feel the same. The call was clear. That afternoon, we returned to Citipointe for their second service, and just like before, as soon as worship began, the tears came, as well as the conviction and clarity.

"This is where I want you to plant," God said.

We both knew it, so we obeyed. We went back to Vineyard, met with the pastors we had served for years, and shared what we were sensing. To their credit, they blessed us and prayed over us. Then they released us.

By the next week, I was sitting quietly in the back of Citipointe, healing, listening, and letting God recalibrate my spirit. I didn't jump into leadership. I knew enough to know I needed to be poured into before I started pouring out again, but after a few weeks, the sense of readiness returned.

I texted Pastor Aaron: "When do you guys need help?"

His reply: "Just show up."

So I did. Week after week, I showed up. I helped set up chairs, ran cables, poured coffee—anything that was needed. I just kept saying yes, and along the way, Aaron began to disciple me. We started sitting down regularly, sharing stories, sharpening each other. He knew my whole story, and rather than distance himself from my past, he leaned in and called it forward.

I couldn't have scripted it better if I tried. The church where I got saved. The youth group where I first heard God's voice. The room where someone once pointed at a teenage kid and said, "You'll be a pastor one day." God brought it all full circle.

THE YEAR OF YES

By the start of 2016, my life was stable on paper. I was off the ankle bracelet, growing in my marriage, working a steady job, and plugged into a new church community. But God wasn't done with me. In fact, He was just getting started.

One day, Pastor Aaron asked me to do the Sunday announcements at Citipointe. It was just a simple, short welcome, nothing flashy, but you would've thought he asked me to give a TED Talk at Madison Square Garden.

Fear flooded back in, the same fear I had as a sixth-grade boy standing in front of the classroom, shaking as I stammered through a report on the human body. My knees buckled. In the past, I would've lied and made an excuse. "I'm sick." "I have something else going on." But I was tired of bowing to fear. That night, I went home, locked myself in a room, and cried out to God.

"If this is what You've called me to, if You want me to speak, then You're going to have to do it in me because there's not a single ounce of me that wants this."

And then came the voice again—the same unmistakable voice I'd heard in prison. God said, "Rick, I just need you to do one thing."

"What's that?" I asked.

"Say yes."

That was it. Not "be fearless." Not "do it perfectly." Just say yes.

So I did. I declared 2016 my "Year of Yes." I told God, "Whatever You put in front of me this year, I'll say yes to it." I laugh now, thinking of how I tried to bargain with the Creator of the universe, as if He needed my permission. "I'll give You a year," I told Him. "Just one." But God didn't laugh. He just started opening doors.

I made those first announcements afraid. My voice shook, my hands trembled, but I got through it. Then came a Tuesday night service where I was asked to lead. I said yes. Only eight people were in the room, but it might as well have been a stadium. Still, I showed up.

Then came a communion message with thirty people in the room. I was so nervous I had to brace my elbows against my ribs to keep my hands from shaking uncontrollably, but again, I said yes.

Each time, the fear lost a little more power. Each time, my confidence grew. I wasn't confident in myself. Rather, I was confident that obedience, not ability, was what God was after. That year, I grew more in my leadership, my calling, and my character than in any other season of my life. God put me on a fast track of growth, but He also taught me something else: *Your story matters but so does timing.*

Coming out of prison, I didn't lead with my past. When I met new people, whether it was my wife's family, coworkers, or members of the church, I let them get to know *me* before I shared my testimony. It's not that I was ashamed, but I understood human nature. Some people hear "prison" and stop listening, but when they knew my heart—when they knew me as a husband, a father, a servant—they were ready to hear the rest.

"Wait, *you* were in prison?" they would ask.

Yes, and *that's* when the story hits differently. Transformation is more powerful when it's proven.

I've come to believe your past doesn't define your future, but it can prepare you for it. With God, *all things are possible*, and with the right people around you, you can rebuild a life that exceeds your imagination. But there's one thing you can't do: live a double life. I've tried it so I know the cost.

I can't pinpoint exactly when it started—maybe when my parents divorced and I had to split my identity between two homes. One version of me at my mom's. Another at my dad's. It became natural to present different versions of myself depending on who was watching, but the only person fooled by a double life is *you*. Everyone else sees it, and even if they don't, *God does*. Double lives always lead to destruction.

If you're reading this, and you're stuck living two lives—one in public, one in private—it's time to come clean. You'll never have peace while your soul is divided. Freedom begins when you become whole.

In coming to Citipointe, I saw that God isn't just in the business of redemption. He's in the business of *restoration*. Full circle restoration. That church where I was saved as a teenager, the one where someone once prophesied that I'd be a pastor, twenty years later, I was back in the same spiritual lineage, now stepping into the very calling that was spoken over my life as a boy.

You can't make that up. You can't manufacture that kind of symmetry. Only God can write a story like that. That's how I know He's real—not just because I believe the Bible, not just because I've felt His presence, but because no human hand could have orchestrated this journey. From four-time felon to pastor, from drug addict to pulpit, from running from God to running with Him.

If you look at your own life closely enough, you'll see the fingerprints too. You'll recall the moments that *shouldn't* have happened but did, the breaks you didn't deserve, the relationships that came full circle, and the doors that opened for you. None of it is chance. You really can find hope in the ashes.

Even now, in my life, the enemy still lurks. He always does, especially when you've come from the darkness. Even in the goodness of these last few years, I've seen his thread trying to weave itself back into my life. Isolation is his favorite tactic. Up in Estes Park, when I was working and living apart from my community, I felt the temptation to slip back into secrecy. That's why community is everything.

Accountability isn't weakness. It's wisdom. Vulnerability is strength. Whether you're a Christian or not, if you want to grow as a person, you need someone who knows *all* of you and who will hold you to your highest standard, not your lowest excuse.

Those were the biggest lessons I learned in those first few years of freedom. Say yes. Live whole. Stay accountable. And never underestimate what God can do with a surrendered life.

CHAPTER NINE

GOD'S CALLING

THE "YEAR OF YES" CHANGED MY LIFE. IT WAS THE YEAR I stopped letting fear drive the car and started letting obedience take the wheel. That posture of surrender launched me, finally, into the calling I had run from since the sixth grade—the calling God whispered into my heart the first time I stood trembling in front of a classroom.

When Lacey and I stepped out in faith to help plant Citipointe Church, the congregation was small—just fifty or so people packed into a dusty, converted warehouse with stained carpets and flickering lights—but God was clearly there. After that first trembling "yes," doors began to open. The church began to grow. I watched in awe as our little body of believers doubled, then doubled again—seventy became 140, then 280. New faces poured in every Sunday. The energy was electric, and the Spirit was moving.

I kept saying yes. Every time I stepped up to that platform, it felt like I was staring down my own personal Goliath. That childhood fear of public speaking, the shame that once silenced me, was still there, but each time I stood up and opened my mouth, I drove the sword a little deeper into the giant's chest.

Those first few years in ministry were beautiful and brutal, a training ground for everything I would become. I learned how to lead, how to listen, how to serve when no one sees, how to carry a vision that wasn't mine but felt like home. There were Sunday mornings I wanted to quit, and Tuesday nights I felt wholly unqualified. But there were also altar calls that broke me open and worship sets that reminded me why I believed in miracles.

What made it harder was that I wasn't on staff. From 2016 to 2020, I served in full-time ministry while also working a full-time job for Matt at M&E Painting. I'd put in fifty hours at my job during the week, then give every spare minute to the church—preaching, setting up chairs, counseling, praying, leading, pouring out. In the midst of all that, I was also raising twin daughters and trying to love my wife well.

It was exhausting, but it was also exhilarating. Something inside me had awakened. I wasn't just helping build a church, I was being built myself. Each moment I chose obedience over comfort, each time I killed fear with faith, I could feel God shaping me into the man He had always seen.

As the years rolled on, the question in my spirit grew louder and clearer: *What if this is what I'm supposed to do full time?*

I didn't have a plan yet. I didn't know how God would make it happen, but I knew the longing was real. I had tasted purpose, and I wanted more. I wanted to give my whole life to ministry, not just my nights and weekends. I didn't want to build someone else's dream by day and God's kingdom by night. I wanted to go all in, and I had a sense deep in my soul that another *yes* was coming.

THE WEIGHT OF ONE

By the end of 2017, Lacey and I began to believe it was possible, just maybe, that we could have another child. The twins were nearly five years old, and the lingering shell shock from those early sleepless nights was finally starting to wear off. For the first time, we looked at each other and thought, *We could do this again.* Not two, though. Just one this time.

That was the catch, of course, because once you've had twins, your chances of having them again go up. As much as we adored our girls, the thought of doubling the chaos a second time was enough to raise our blood pressure on the spot. So, we entered this new season of trying with equal parts faith and caution, hoping for one more blessing but not two.

When Lacey got pregnant, we were thrilled but nervous all over again. The day of our twenty-four-week ultrasound, we sat in the car outside the clinic, having the same back-and-forth we'd had in whispers for weeks.

"If it's twins again," I told her, "you're going to have to quit your job. I'll work two jobs. You stay home with the kids. We'll figure it out."

It was a conversation laced with love and humor, but a very real kind of fear. We were suffering from a bad case of PTTSD (post-traumatic twins stress disorder)!

Finally, we walked into the clinic, and I was ready.

"Listen," I told the technician. "Don't get clever. Don't say anything about two heads. Just tell us straight—how many, and what is it?"

She smiled and looked up from the screen. "It's one," she said, "and it's a boy."

Lacey and I both exhaled at once. Relief and joy hit like a tidal wave. We'd both dreamed of having a son to complete the picture, a boy to grow up beside our girls. It felt perfect. Two daughters, one son, and us.

But as quickly as the joy came, it was chased by something

else: the weight of fatherly responsibility. All the old memories came flooding back. My dad, his temper, his failures. The good, the bad, the broken. I realized at that moment that I was being given a chance to father differently—to break the cycle.

Strangely, I found myself feeling a new kind of respect for my dad. As flawed as he was, he had shown me something valuable even in the absence of what I needed. In a backward way, he taught me how *not* to father, and that, too, was a lesson I could use.

Weeks later, at church, a friend prayed over me. "I believe God's going to show you something powerful about your son's birth," he said. I thanked him, but I didn't give it much thought.

Then came the delivery day. We scheduled it for convenience. I wasn't working, Lacey could rest, and it landed on a weekend. Josiah was born via C-section, and he was healthy, strong, and *massive*. He weighed as much as the twins had *combined*. It was like carrying two babies again, but all in one.

And then it hit me. He was born on August 28, 2018.

8-28-18.

Romans 8:28 says, "And we know that in all things God works for the good of those who love him, who are called according to his purpose."

If you've ever studied biblical numerology, you might know that the number eight signifies *new beginnings*. At the time, I didn't think much of it, until God brought it all together as I was sitting in the recovery room that evening.

Josiah's birth wasn't just a new chapter but a declaration. God was working *all* things together for good, even the pain, the mistakes, and the broken legacy I once feared I'd pass down. This was the grace of God, bundled in nine pounds and eight ounces of purpose.

Josiah was more than a child—he was a sign. He was God's stamp of redemption on my life. Every step I had taken, through the prison sentence, the addictions, the broken relationships, the silent cries at night, all of it had led to this moment. It wasn't in vain or wasted time. *Everything had worked together for good.*

Even his name said it all. *Josiah*, in Hebrew, means *Jehovah has healed*. Past tense. Not *He will heal*, but *He has healed*. His very name was a declaration that God had reached back into the mess of my past and rewoven it into something beautiful.

I looked at Josiah, then to my daughters, then to Lacey, and I felt God's grace settle over me. After everything I'd been through, after all I had done and left undone, here I was: not just a man, but a father, a husband, and a spiritual leader. I was not defined by my past but redeemed through it.

I get choked up even now writing about it because for so long, I never thought I'd make it this far, much less with a family like this. God did what only He can do. He didn't just forgive me, He *healed* me. The prophecy my dad spoke over me when I got locked up in Kansas finally came to pass.

Now, I get to be the dad who protects, who teaches and loves. I get to be the kind of father I didn't have growing up. The kind of father who stays and prays, who breaks the curse and starts a new legacy.

God didn't just give me a son, he gave me a new beginning, and He signed it with the numbers *8.28.18*.

LAST CALL

Josiah's birth was a moment of deep joy and profound redemption in my life, but it wasn't without pain. You see, when Josiah was born—my only son, my legacy—my father never came to see him. There was no hospital visit or phone call, just a text message that said, *Congratulations*. That was it. For some reason, that hurt more than I expected it to. I tried to brush it off, but in my heart, I knew something was off.

Months passed, and we entered the last day of 2018. It was

New Year's Eve, and we were at a church service. Just as we were stepping into a new year with anticipation, I got the call.

My dad was in the hospital. There was something in me that just *knew*. I can't explain it, but my spirit recognized the finality in the moment. The Holy Spirit whispered a reminder to me, a truth I'd tried to forget: *He's going to drink himself to death.* I remembered the time back in 2008 when he'd relapsed after years of sobriety. That day, I felt it deep in my bones that this road would end in tragedy if he didn't turn around, and now, ten years later, the road had run out.

Before leaving church to go see him, I asked one of my closest friends to pray over me. As he did, he paused, then said with startling clarity, "Rick, I'm sorry, but I hear the Lord saying: *Last call.*"

He had no idea about my dad's addiction. He didn't know the years of battles with alcohol, the relapses, the pain, but that phrase—*last call*—hit like a freight train. If you've ever been to a bar at closing time, you know what it means. Last chance. Last drink. No more refills. Time's up. I knew it was a word from God.

When I arrived at the hospital in Denver, I hardly recognized my dad. He was bloated, pale, and distant. We hadn't really spoken in years. In my experience, that was always a sign that things weren't going well with him. He'd go quiet when he was drinking again and withdrawing from everyone—especially me.

I sat with him. I talked and prayed, but he wouldn't tell me what was really going on. For days, I went back and forth to the hospital. Doctors wouldn't tell me much, and my dad kept deflecting.

"It's just diverticulitis," he'd say. "They're trying dialysis. I'll be fine."

I knew better, and eventually, someone told me the truth. His liver had gone into full cirrhosis. Years of alcohol abuse had destroyed it. The liver failure had cascaded into kidney failure, which meant his body couldn't filter toxins or fight infections, and he had a bad infection in his intestines.

The infection had taken hold and was spreading. His organs couldn't stop it. There was only one option left: a last-ditch surgery to try and remove the infected section of his intestines.

I waited, praying and hoping. An hour later, the surgeon came out, face heavy with sorrow. "There's nothing we can do," he said. "The infection is so severe it's actually starting to melt the tissue. We can't remove it. I'm sorry."

The finality of it pierced through me like a knife. I had sensed it coming. I had heard the voice of the Lord, but hearing it out loud—*There's nothing we can do*—left me breathless.

My dad didn't have a will and had no power of attorney. His house was in pre-foreclosure, and some sleazy real estate agent was circling like a vulture, trying to take advantage of his condition to snatch it away. I had to step in. The hospital transferred him to hospice, and what followed were the two longest weeks of my life.

I barely slept. Hospice care is holy, brutal ground. It's where you go to wait. Where the clock ticks differently. Where silence is deafening and memories become your only conversation. I sat with my dad every day, watching the man who raised me, the man who wounded me, the man who never came to see my son, slip away piece by piece.

I was heartbroken and exhausted. At times, I was incredibly angry, but I was also grateful because God had prepared me. He gave me time to be with him. Time to forgive him. To carry the weight of his exit and hand it back to the One who carries us all. This was my father's *last call*.

THE FINAL CONVERSATION

The end came slowly, and painfully. We had to move my father midway through hospice care because the first facility just wasn't doing their job. It was overwhelming trying to manage the logistics, the legal mess, and the emotional toll of watching someone die, all at once. Somewhere between his moments of lucidity and slipping into comas, we were trying to talk about wills and property and what would happen to the house when he passed. It was surreal, grappling with death while trying to tie up the loose ends of a life.

I was the one holding it all together, my dad's only biological son. I had always carried an unspoken sense of responsibility, and in those final days, it became clear that this was mine to carry, all of it.

I remember the night my dad slipped into his final coma. He was restless and agitated. He kept trying to sit up, to stand, to move, over and over. Finally, I snapped.

"Dad, you've got to stop. You're going to fall and hurt yourself."

I raised my voice—something I regret now. He looked at me with a stubborn, pleading expression, and I could see it in his eyes: *If I don't get up, I'm going to die.*

He didn't want to die, but that night, he stopped trying. That night, the coma took hold. He lingered for over a week, and for anyone who's walked with a loved one through hospice, you know the waiting is agonizing. You feel helpless and totally exhausted. By day five, I had hit my limit. I told myself I just needed to go home, get a shower, sleep a little, clear my head. I thought, *Maybe if I can just work a few hours tomorrow, I'll feel normal again.*

The next morning, I woke up feeling almost human. I made it to work. Thirty minutes into my shift, the call came. My father was gone.

Later I learned what often happens in hospice is that people wait to die until they're alone. It's as if they don't want their family to bear witness. That was true for my dad. Even his wife, Paula, had stepped away for a quick shower. In that brief, quiet moment, he slipped away.

I felt so many things—grief, certainly, but also an unexpected sense of relief. The long battle was over.

I was deeply grateful that before he slipped into the coma, we'd had one last real conversation. When the doctors told us there was nothing else they could do, I asked everyone to leave the room. I needed one final moment. Just me and my dad. That's when he looked at me, tired and hollow-eyed, and said, "Rick, I'm sorry. I didn't know how to be a dad. I never had one."

It was the first and last time I ever heard him say those words.

In that moment, something broke inside me. The pain I had carried for years—the resentment, the anger, the ache of not being fathered—just dissolved. I saw him not as the man who failed me, but as a broken son himself, and I forgave him.

We cried. We hugged. He also recommitted his life to Christ that day. We prayed together, and I believe with all my heart I'll see him again one day, whole and healed.

I could've walked away. I had every reason to say, "You weren't there for me—why should I be there for you?" But I didn't. I stayed, and I'm so thankful I did. Shortly after that conversation, he slipped into a coma and never came out of it.

When I got the news he had passed, I picked up my little sister, Kathryn, and we went back to the hospice. There were still balloons in the room that my older sister, Adriana, had brought when he first arrived. They'd somehow lasted an entire month, floating quietly like sentinels of time.

I braced myself to see his body, but to my surprise, it didn't shake me like I thought it would. What I saw wasn't my dad—it was just a shell. He was gone, really gone. My sister and I stood together, and then something in me knew what we needed to do. I opened the door, and we let the balloons go. As they drifted up into the winter sky, it felt like we were releasing him, saying, "You can go now, Dad. We're going to be okay."

There was peace in the room after that. We held his hand

one last time. Then we gathered his things and left. His body was cremated soon after.

I told myself it was over. That I could now get back to life. But grief doesn't work like that. It waits for you, and I was about to learn that letting go of a person doesn't mean you're done healing from the years they couldn't be who you needed them to be.

THE FATHER WOUND

In the months that followed my dad's death, there was little time to grieve. I was scrambling to save his house from foreclosure, pulling money from my own savings just to keep things afloat. His wife and my little sister were still living there, and I was doing everything I could to make sure they were taken care of. But the financial reality was clear: We had to sell.

Finally, I sat down with them and had the hard conversation.

"By the end of February," I said, "you'll need to be out of the house."

It wasn't easy, but they understood. We got the house listed, sold it, and—by the grace of God—there was just enough to cover the bills, reimburse what I'd put in, and give each of the siblings a small inheritance check. That part felt redemptive, like I had done right by my dad, even at the end. I was proud of that.

After that, I thought life would pick up again. That we'd bury him, settle, and move on, but instead, I began to spiral. It wasn't dramatic or obvious at first, just a subtle, steady collapse. Suddenly, I didn't want to pray. I didn't want to read Scripture. I wasn't hearing from God. I felt far away, and for the first time in my life, I didn't know who I was.

Losing a parent does something to you. For some, it's sorrow. For others, it's relief. For me, it was identity loss. My father's passing left a hole, not just in my life but in my sense of self. For as long as I could remember, I'd been trying to prove something to him. I wanted to prove I didn't need him, that I could do it without him, and now, with him gone, I had no one left to prove anything to. I had no idea how empty that would feel.

One afternoon, I found myself in a coffee shop in Fort Collins, sobbing. I was just sitting at a table, broken, with other customers looking at me like I'd lost my mind. Maybe I had. I pounded my fist on the table and cried out, "What do you want from me, God?"

And then it happened again. That voice. The same still, small voice I'd heard in the prison cell, in the silence when I had no more prayers left to pray.

He said, "Rick, I just want you to be my son."

Suddenly, everything came into focus. My entire relationship with God up until then had been through a broken filter. I had projected the image of my earthly father onto my Heavenly Father. I thought I had to perform to be accepted. I thought I had to achieve to be loved.

But here was God inviting me not to strive but to simply *be* His son. Finally, I understood what sonship really meant. Theologians and counselors talk about something called the "father wound." It's a deep ache, an unspoken grief many men carry when their earthly fathers are absent, abusive, or emotionally unavailable. It's a wound that warps your sense of identity. You drag it with you into adulthood, into marriage, into fatherhood, into ministry.

Sitting there in that coffee shop, I felt it heal. God wasn't asking me to prove anything. He wasn't demanding performance. He was just offering love and identity.

You're my son.

That truth rewired how I approached ministry. It transformed how I fathered my own kids. It healed a part of me I didn't realize was still bleeding. I could finally love my son not from a place of reaction or fear, but from a place of freedom. I could pass on identity to him in a way that had never been passed on to me.

I no longer lived as an orphan trying to earn approval. I lived as a son who was accepted, secure, and already loved. And from that place, everything began to heal.

TWO YEARS AND A DREAM

Through all of this joy, heartache, and struggle, I was being pulled into ministry.

It was sometime in late 2018, right around the time my son Josiah was born, when I first started to feel a deep longing to move into full-time ministry. I was already doing ministry almost full time, but I wasn't being paid for it. I was still working as a project manager for M&E Painting, running job sites, overseeing teams, and balancing schedules, all while pouring myself into the church. I was stretched thin, but something inside me knew this was more than just passion—it was a calling.

So I started praying, asking God, "When? When can I do this full time? When can I leave the day job and give my life completely to the ministry?"

And then I heard his response as clear as day: "In two years."

Two years? I remember thinking, *That's so long.* I wanted to jump in then and there, but I knew better. I'd learned enough by that point to trust God's timeline, not my own, so I buckled down and kept going.

Fast-forward to the summer of 2019, nearly a year and a half later. I was counting the months. *Could this be it? Could this be the moment He was preparing me for?*

That's when Pastor Aaron pulled me aside and said, "I think it's time. We'd like to bring you on full time."

I could hardly believe it, but before I could say yes, I knew I needed to have a conversation with my boss, Matt. He had become one of the most influential men in my life. I had told him from the start, "I will never leave this job unless it's to become a pastor."

Matt didn't flinch. In fact, he offered to pay for something called a *StratOp Life Plan,* a two-day experience designed to help you map your story, clarify your purpose, and discern your next move. It wasn't cheap, but Matt believed in investing in people. That's just who he is. He wanted me to be sure, so I did it.

We spread my life across whiteboards and timelines. We dug through the patterns of my past, the moments of breakthrough, the wounds and the wins, and by the end of those two days, everything inside me said yes. Yes to the call. Yes to the next chapter. Yes to full-time ministry.

When I told Matt, he shook my hand and blessed me. We planned a six-month transition, and I began training my replacement.

Finally, in September 2019, I stood on the platform at Citipointe Church with pastors surrounding me. They laid hands on me, prayed over me, and right there, during the ordination, I heard it again—another divine reminder. It was the prophecy from when I was fifteen years old, when Pastor Mark Ramsey spoke over me at Center Point Church and said one day I'd be a pastor. Here I was, twenty years later, in one of Pastor Mark's churches, being ordained into the very call spoken over me two decades prior.

God had fulfilled His promises.

January 4, 2020, was my first official day as a full-time pastor. It felt like a dream. From felonies and addiction, from prison and brokenness, to an office at a church, a key to the building, and a calling that finally had a home.

And then, two months later, the whole world shut down.

COVID-19 hit. Churches everywhere went dark. The days of lockdowns, fear, and scrambling for toilet paper were upon us. I remember watching the news as the first case entered the US, then watching it sweep across the country. I thought to myself, *Seriously? I just got here. This is what ministry is going to be like?*

But God simply said, *Be faithful.*

And we were. We adapted. We did online services, held drive-in services in the parking lot, even hosted a church gathering at a local drive-in movie theater. We partnered with a local restaurant, Betta Gumbo, and started serving free meals to the community. More than ten thousand meals were served during the height of the pandemic.

God's faithfulness didn't stop when the doors closed. If anything, He multiplied it. Something else happened as well. Our church took a bold stand during that time to keep having services, and people started showing up in droves. Hundreds came, then hundreds more. In a time when many churches were shrinking, we were growing.

In January 2022, two years into my staff role, I was promoted to executive pastor, second in line. I was now responsible for teams, systems, and strategy, but also for souls. The responsibility was intense, but so was the joy.

There were some big milestones: the first Sunday I preached. Then the first time I preached back-to-back weekends. Then came leadership responsibilities, staff hires, tough conversations, moments of burnout, moments of breakthrough. Through it all, God kept stretching me, refining me, shaping me into a better leader.

As I write this, I just celebrated five years on staff. Five years in full-time ministry. Five years since I stepped into the calling that had been whispered over me at fifteen. And I've learned that God never forgets what He promised—even when we run. Even when we fail. Even when the world shuts down.

He is always faithful to finish what He starts.

A HOME FOR REDEMPTION

There's one more thing I need to mention. Sometimes, God's provision surprises us in the most generous, humbling ways.

It was Father's Day 2019. We were at my wife's parents'

home, sitting around the table after a meal. Her dad slid an envelope across the table toward us. Inside was the deed to the house we'd been renting from them. No strings attached. Just a gift. I'll never forget that moment. I remember thinking: *This isn't just generosity. This is redemption.*

Lacey's father had already paid for the remainder of her master's degree. Now, they were giving us the roof over our heads. And then, after her aunt passed recently, Lacey received an inheritance that completely changed our financial situation.

Here I am, a boy who grew up in brokenness and poverty, sitting in the kind of home I used to stare at from the street and wonder, *What do those people do for a living?* Now I'm one of those people. Sitting in my home office, surrounded by my wife, my children, and the presence of God—that's not luck, that's grace.

We didn't get here alone. In 2017, my mother—who had long been entangled in addiction and spiritual confusion—called me and said she was done. *Done with her old life. Ready for something new.* We moved her into our home, got her cleaned up, loved on her, and brought her to church. She surrendered her life to Christ, and she's been following Him with full devotion ever since. These days, she has her own place, her own income, and her dignity back. Every Sunday, she sits next to me in church. She is one of my biggest supporters, and her story is one of the most beautiful redemptions I've ever witnessed.

My brother, after three combat tours in Iraq, came home broken too, but now—after a long stay at a PTSD recovery home—he's doing better. He's finding himself again. And my two younger sisters are both serving in the navy, making something of their lives.

Not every story wrapped up neatly, though. My oldest sister is still on the streets. She comes and goes. When she visits, I love her fiercely. I tell her about Jesus every chance I get, but then she disappears again. I pray for her constantly.

Then there's Paula. After I had to ask her to leave the house, her life fell apart. I gave her opportunities, but she chose a different path, and eventually, she ended up homeless. One day, I got a call from the police. They found her dead from an overdose. Just like that, she was gone.

It breaks my heart for my three youngest sisters. They've now lost both parents. Paula may have been absent, but she was still *Mom*. And my dad, though flawed and broken, had tried, in the end, to be something for them. Now he's gone too, and those girls are left trying to navigate life without the guidance of a mother or father.

We do what we can, especially for the youngest. She's special to us. She's still trying to find her way, still working through grief and growing pains. We're giving her space to be an adult, but she knows we're here. She knows she's loved.

So here's where I sit now. I'm in a home I never thought I'd own, surrounded by stories of pain and healing, loss and redemption. I think about my journey often. From prison cells and drug deals to pulpits and prayer meetings. From a father's abandonment to my Father's embrace. From being the one who always needed help to now being the one who helps.

Maybe that's the point. You don't get to choose where you start, but you do get to choose who you trust to carry you forward. I've chosen to trust the One who was with me in the jail cell, in the halfway house, in the NICU, at the funeral home, and right here in my office today.

He's the reason I'm still here. He's the reason I'll keep going. And He's not finished yet.

CONCLUSION

ONE MORE LIFE AT A TIME

I BELIEVE WITH ALL MY HEART THAT EVERYTHING CHANGES the moment you stop running.

When you stop running from your calling, when you stop hiding from that whisper deep in your soul that tells you what you were made to do, life begins to take shape. Things start to fall into place because you're finally walking in rhythm with your purpose.

For years, I resisted the prophecy spoken over me as a teenager. I denied it, ran from it, convinced myself I could chart my own course. I told God, "You don't get to dictate who I become." But I had it backward. God wasn't forcing me into anything. He had formed me for it. He didn't impose purpose onto me; He had created me *with* purpose, *for* purpose.

Everything changed in 2016. That year, I made a simple but life-altering vow to say yes to God—yes to everything He asked of me. No matter how uncomfortable or terrifying it felt, I said yes. That one year became the catalyst that set off a chain reaction. Doors opened, hearts healed, opportunities appeared, and I found myself standing in places I once thought were unreachable.

I know this is still only the beginning. Loss, I've come to realize, is often the turning point for transformation. When I lost my dad, I didn't just bury a parent, I unlocked a part of myself that had been buried for years. His death shattered something in me, but in the breaking, something else was released. The orphaned boy inside me was finally allowed to grow up, and the man I am today emerged. That man is a father to his children in a way my father never could be to me.

When I look back over the whole story, I can trace God's fingerprints in every chapter. The times He provided. The moments He protected. The doors He opened when I didn't know which way to turn. If you go back to the beginning of this story, you'll see them too—those divine interruptions that changed everything.

But there's one name that deserves to be spoken again, and it seems fitting to close this book by honoring him one more time. He is the person whose life marked mine forever: Steven.

Every time I tell my story, I come back to him. Steven didn't have to die, and I will never be able to undo the moment that I took his life. I carry that pain every day. It's part of my story, and I will never pretend otherwise. What I've come to realize over time—what humbles me deeply—is that in some mysterious, painful way, Steven's death became the event that saved my life.

He never knew me. He never meant to give his life for mine, nor should he have had to. I have vowed that I will not let that loss be in vain. If I can reach one more person—just *one more*—if I can help change even one more life for the better, then there is meaning woven into the tragedy. There is legacy born from the wreckage. There is a ripple effect, started by one moment of heartbreak, that can stretch across generations.

So, ultimately, this book is for Steven. He is not a footnote in my testimony but a central turning point. That night changed everything and forced me to see what I had become. It lit the path for who I was meant to be.

Steven, you mattered. You still do. Your legacy lives on, one more life at a time.

To the readers of this book: Thank you for following me on this journey. It has been a long one, but the journey doesn't have to stop here for you. In fact, it can begin. I want to extend an invitation and a prayer: Stop running and start listening to that still, small voice. The Lord is not mad at you. He loves and cares about you deeply. Your life might be one prayer away from a total transformation. If you're ready to make that decision now, you can pray this simple prayer:

Lord Jesus, please forgive me of my sins. I repent and turn away from them and commit my life to you now. I ask that you would fill me up with your Spirit, and I declare from this day forward, I am now a child of God. Amen.

If you prayed that from your heart, I want to congratulate you and welcome you into the family of God! This is the first step in a lifelong journey of faith. I encourage you to share your decision with someone, find a local church, and surround yourself with people who will encourage and support you. Make God's Word a daily priority—download the YouVersion Bible app and start a reading plan today.

May the Lord bless you and keep you, may His face shine upon you and be gracious to you, and may He fill you with peace as you walk with Him from this day forward. In Jesus's name, amen.

ABOUT THE AUTHOR

RICK SCADDEN is the executive pastor at Citipointe Church Northern Colorado in Loveland, Colorado. His life is a powerful testament of transformation, redemption, and the unwavering grace of God.

Born into a world of poverty, addiction, and instability, Rick's early years were marked by chaos and hardship. By his early twenties, he had accumulated four felony convictions, leading to a prison sentence that became a major turning point in his life. It was within the confines of his cell that Rick experienced a profound spiritual awakening, responding to God's call and embarking on a journey of faith and renewal.

Upon his release, Rick committed himself wholeheartedly to his spiritual growth and calling. He became actively involved in his local church, eventually joining the staff at Citipointe Church Northern Colorado. Through faith and perseverance, he rose to the position of executive pastor, where he now leads with compassion and a deep understanding of God's grace.

Beyond his pastoral duties, Rick is a devoted husband to his wife, Lacey, and a loving father to their three children: Sadie, Amariah, and Josiah.

www.ingramcontent.com/pod-product-compliance
Lightning Source LLC
Chambersburg PA
CBHW060525080526
44586CB00012B/621